# PRAISE FOR *BETTER BROKEN*

"Sean nailed it with *Better Broken*! He's a living example of how a life of adversity can become your greatest advantage. This is the manual for anyone who is ready to turn their mess into their message."
—**Bedros Keuilian, entrepreneur and author of *Man Up***

"Trauma doesn't have to limit or define you. Rooted in real-world experience and a clear-eyed philosophy, Sean Rogers offers a practical approach for reframing hardship for self-mastery."
—**Scott Barry Kaufman, PhD, cognitive scientist and author of *Transcend* and *Choose Growth***

"Fascinating, well-written, and meticulously researched, *Better Broken* is a joyous road map for fulfillment. Traumatized or not, I urge you to read it to better understand yourself and those around you. A wonderfully important book."
—**Jonny Lee Miller, actor and firefighter**

# BETTER BROKEN

**ALSO BY SEAN J. ROGERS**

*Rising Above*

# BETTER BROKEN

## The Hidden Advantage of a Challenging Life

**SEAN J. ROGERS**

BenBella Books, Inc.
Dallas, TX

This book is for informational purposes only. It is not intended to serve as a substitute for professional medical advice. The author and publisher specifically disclaim any and all liability arising directly or indirectly from the use of any information contained in this book. A health care professional should be consulted regarding your specific medical situation. Any product mentioned in this book does not imply endorsement of that product by the author or publisher.

*Better Broken* copyright © 2024 by Sean J. Rogers

All rights reserved. No part of this book may be used or reproduced in any manner whatsoever without written permission of the publisher, except in the case of brief quotations embodied in critical articles or reviews.

BenBella Books, Inc.
10440 N. Central Expressway
Suite 800
Dallas, TX 75231
benbellabooks.com
Send feedback to feedback@benbellabooks.com

*BenBella* is a federally registered trademark.

Printed in the United States of America
10 9 8 7 6 5 4 3 2 1

Library of Congress Control Number: 2023024300
ISBN 9781637743867 (hardcover)
ISBN 9781637743874 (electronic)

Editing by Glenn Yeffeth and Joe Rhatigan
Copyediting by Michael Fedison
Proofreading by Jenny Bridges and Cape Cod Compositors, Inc.
Text design and composition by Aaron Edmiston
Cover design by Brigid Pearson
Printed by Lake Book Manufacturing

Special discounts for bulk sales are available.
Please contact bulkorders@benbellabooks.com.

This book is dedicated to my beautiful wife Pamela
and our two daughters, Mia and Maliah.

To my girls:

Let this book be a reminder that the cycle of abuse was broken in our family. The only expectation I have of either of you is to keep it that way. Understand that my admiration and love for you will never be something that needs to be earned; it was given the day you were born.

Chase the things you love no matter what. Following your heart will bring you more joy and appreciation for life than any title or number in a bank account.

The Bible is the best self-help book ever created, read it.

Lastly, never let a day pass without telling someone you love them. Preferably your mom and I, but I guess one day a spouse as well . . . but mostly your mom and me.

Love always,

Dad

# CONTENTS

Introduction ................................... 1

**Chapter 1**  The Beginning ........................... 5
**Chapter 2**  Transitioning from Surviving to Succeeding ......... 17
**Chapter 3**  Recognizing and Analyzing Your Triggers .......... 35
**Chapter 4**  Eliminate Negativity ...................... 49
**Chapter 5**  Rejection Is Okay ........................ 61
**Chapter 6**  Forgiveness Is Key ....................... 67
**Chapter 7**  The Victim ............................ 79
**Chapter 8**  Financial Pitfalls ........................ 97
**Chapter 9**  Power of Reading ....................... 109
**Chapter 10** Journaling ............................ 119
**Chapter 11** The Confidence of a Fit Body ............... 131
**Chapter 12** One Thing at a Time ..................... 143
**Chapter 13** On Goals and Failure .................... 157
**Chapter 14** Success, and How to Define It .............. 167
**Chapter 15** Consistency / Building Habits .............. 179
**Chapter 16** Build the Life You Want .................. 189

Notes ...................................... 195

# INTRODUCTION

Every day, thousands of children are neglected, abandoned, and abused. They suffer from their parents' or guardians' poor life choices and are often left to navigate their way into adulthood with all the baggage that comes with surviving hardship. These children grow up dealing with post-traumatic stress disorders, anxiety disorders, and lists of mental and physical health issues.

Some of these children will grow up embittered by the unfairness of their circumstances and use their trauma as an excuse to hurt others and avoid responsibility. They will stumble through life unable to get out of their own way. Their failed attempts will only confirm their bias that the world is against them.

Yet, others will figure out how to transition their trauma into success. When they do, they will find it on a scale most will never experience. It will appear to everyone else that they are gifted or special in some unexplainable way. They will have a drive, charisma, and focus that are unparalleled. These "broken" people who emerge from trauma to great success do so because of their trauma. They have learned to harness their trauma and utilize it.

This book is a guide for those who have suffered . . . for those "broken" people who feel lost and unseen . . . for those kids whose parents failed to teach them how to achieve. It is a road map to transition from poverty and abuse to unstoppable success. If you are "broken" like me (and I use that term proudly), this book will help you learn to hone your trauma, control your response to triggers, and unleash the power that accompanies your pain. And if you are already achieving, then I hope this book not only gives you support to keep on succeeding but also encourages you to pass on the lessons you have learned.

I'm here to show that the broken are far more powerful and capable than they can imagine. We understand the world in a different way . . . our trauma has removed the rose-tinted lenses and given us real-world skills and perspectives, and we are only limited by a lack of fundamental habits we were never taught. The principles in this book will help you change your path and skyrocket you to success.

I have spent years practicing and refining these recommendations. In fact, I have failed so many times to master the lessons in this book. The story goes that Thomas Edison tried refining the light bulb 999 times before getting it right the thousandth time. I have made a similar number of attempts to control my reactions to triggers and to use my trauma for good, and I hope that my struggles help you avoid some of my mistakes and reduce the number of attempts to find the success you want.

Finally, I truly believe that it is not enough to transition from poverty and find success. There are millions of children who don't know they are special and that their trauma is better than the most prestigious college degree. They don't know they are primed for success because of their hardships. They feel lost, abandoned, and helpless and are left to think that they have no chance at success or happiness. We owe it to them to prove these defeating thoughts wrong.

Your success is primed and ready, and a few habitual adjustments and mindset shifts will help you counter the years of abuse and psychological trauma.

## By the Numbers

In order to understand just how much work needs to be done, let's dive into the severity of the problem.

Data from the American Society for the Positive Care of Children (ASPCC):[1]

- Fourteen percent of all men in prison and 36 percent of women in prison in the U.S. were abused as children, about twice the frequency seen in the general population.
- Children who experience child abuse and neglect are approximately nine times more likely to become involved in criminal activity.
- Information from the Centers for Disease Control and Prevention (CDC)[2,3]:
  - One out of seven children have experienced child abuse or neglect in the past year, and that number is likely a lot higher when you factor in unreported cases.

- In 2020, 1,750 children died of abuse and neglect in the United States.
- The chances of a child experiencing neglect and abuse is five times higher when they are of a "low socioeconomic status."
- The CDC has coined the term "ACEs," or Adverse Childhood Experiences, that occur in childhood (up to age seventeen). Examples of ACEs include experiencing violence, abuse, or neglect, witnessing violence in the home or community, substance abuse, mental health, and instability due to parental separation.
- Sixty-one percent of adults surveyed across twenty-five states had experienced at least one type of ACE before age eighteen.
- One in six reported that they had experienced four or more types of ACEs.
- The CDC also paints a dire picture for the survivors of child abuse and neglect. The negative news continues regarding the long-term effects for victims, which include: "Increased risk of experiencing future violence victimization and perpetration, substance abuse, sexually transmitted infections, delayed brain development, lower educational attainment, and limited employment opportunities."

## Chapter 1

# THE BEGINNING

*"Most of the important things in the world have been accomplished by people who have kept on trying when there seemed to be no hope at all."*
**–Dale Carnegie**

Before we start, it is important that I give you some background on my childhood and how I got where I am now. You need to understand that I am one of you. I am not a psychologist; I did not get these principles and ideas from books and lectures alone. I am a broken person who learned to transition my trauma into success.

My success is less from the titles I have obtained and more about the love and safety I have cultivated in my home. My greatest source of pride comes from breaking the cycle of abuse and watching my children flourish. However, some of the accomplishments I have achieved with these principles include becoming a Green Beret and then a police officer, earning a master's degree, and becoming an ultra-marathon runner, a bestselling author, and an entrepreneur. No achievement can be truly appreciated without first understanding what it took to get there. This was my beginning; this was the hell where my roots were planted.

..................................

I never grasped the idea that I was missing my father. He left when I was one, and that was that. I never talked to him, never talked about him, and I never even wondered where he was until I was fourteen. Meanwhile, I had plenty of problems to deal with on my own, the first being growing up in the small desert town of Phelan, California. And that, alone, was no easy task.

If you have ever driven from Los Angeles to Las Vegas, you know exactly what I mean. As you pass the hours of endless flat roads surrounded by barren desert, you will see small towns off in the distance. These small towns are seemingly cut off from the rest of the world and surrounded by nothing but lifeless desert and under constant attack from the blazing sun.

The landscape is almost entirely a depressing shade of brown. Even road signs cannot withstand the baking sun. Everything is slowly and surely beaten into submission by the heat. The abundance of tumbleweeds, dust devils, and the little thorns called "stickers" is comical. This is Phelan.

The desert creates a toughness in people. If you don't become tough in the desert, it will make you weird. I don't know if it is the remoteness, the sun, or the people who decide to inhabit that place for life, but most people are affected one way or another.

Desert people are easy to spot ... black, flat-brimmed hats baked slightly brown, Dickies, and puffy-tongued skateboard shoes.

I recently went back to Phelan, hoping to see some change. I saw the same donut shop/Chinese food store I frequented as a kid. The Stater Brothers grocery store still stands completely unchanged. Not a single store had a fresh coat of paint, not one new sign that I could find. Not one hint of change in the entire place. I could still picture skateboarding and fighting behind the Stater Brothers as though time had frozen still.

Stater Brothers was our linkup spot for after-school fistfights. Everyone would walk down from our high school in a mob. Two people would be nervously planning out their attack while the twenty to thirty onlookers buzzed with excitement. Behind the grocery store was a long concrete wall with a ledge that acted as a bench. It was the perfect place to hold our makeshift fight matches.

One afternoon, a large mob met up after the bell rang. We all walked down together taking bets. That day's fight was between two girls. I didn't even know why they wanted to fight; I just saw the mob and followed it. I knew the brother of one of the girls. He is currently serving life in prison for attempted murder. We knew even back then that his family did not play, so I put my money on the sister, Lia.

Before the fight, Lia had one request. She calmly stated, "Don't pull my hair," as though making rules before a fight was normal behavior. Her opponent agreed. Two seconds into the fight, her opponent pulled her hair. You could see Lia's face go from calm to pure rage. She reached up and grabbed a fistful of the other girl's hair with her left hand. Lia swirled the hair in her hand until her opponent's head was tight to her fist. Then with her opposite hand she uppercut the girl in the mouth. Lia continued this pattern repeatedly. With each strike she angrily muttered, "I (punch to the lips) told (punch to the nose) you (punch to the lips)," until she had reiterated their full previous agreement. The fight was over after that. Her opponent unfortunately had a mouth full of braces and spent the next twenty minutes peeling her lips apart from the brackets.

Sure, there were a lot of people who did well in Phelan, but it was as though they lived on a different planet. We were the kids of the poor, the single-family homes, the sons and daughters of drunks, drug addicts, and gang members. Nobody outside of this poverty level seemed to exist to us. How could they? They had no idea what we were going through and they would never understand how we lived.

The broken kids gravitated toward each other, looking for acceptance and understanding. We didn't judge each other. *Your mom drinks a fifth of vodka a day?* All good. Mine drove her car into the house. *Your dad beats your mom?* No judgment from me. I've watched my mom's boyfriend smash her head into the wall. *Your parents don't pay attention to you because they are busy with their own addictions?* What else is new? My mother rarely wakes up unless it is the first of the month when her welfare check arrives.

There were unwritten rules for hanging out with other broken kids. You don't ask questions. You don't pry into their issues. You don't tell them about yours. If people knew how we lived, child protective services would take us away. From a young age, we all felt threatened by child protective services. They were the bad guys that pulled families apart. My mother constantly told me that my siblings would go with strangers and be abused if they were taken away.

It didn't help that some of our friends were in halfway homes, and we could see what the system did with them; they ended up back in the desert living with people just as bad as our parents. These halfway homes were an opportunity for people to make money. The adults were using the system and didn't care about us or our problems. One of the guys we ran with was living in a halfway house as a form of rehab. He was drunk and/or high every time I saw him. He knew what the deal was; he knew they didn't care about him.

We broken kids, often lonely and starving for attention, had a level of freedom that was unparalleled. We were more independent than most adults. And with that independence, we learned the realities and harshness of life early on. We had no illusions about what the world could dish out. We could see that it was either get with the program or get left behind.

- - -

Growing up poor in a broken home was hell on earth for me. I wanted to escape it so badly. Looking back on my childhood, I realized that I lacked two things every child should have: safety and love. And honestly, I would have settled just for safety. My home was terrifying, and there was always something happening. The drunken fights were the scariest times of my life. Even to this day, after having survived combat and police riots, my mother and her boyfriend's fights take the cake.

It was always the same pattern. The drinking started in the early afternoon. After hours of hard drinking, one of them would say something that irritated the other. Then the arguing started. The volume of the argument would grow louder and louder until they were in a screaming match, neither of them listening to a word the other was saying. In the beginning, I tried to intervene, hoping to diffuse the situation. This typically just made me a target, so I opted for avoidance instead.

Shortly after the screaming started, I would find myself hiding in a closet. Before long, the sound of shattering plates and glasses would fill the house. The thuds of tables getting flipped and walls being punched. I would sit in the closet trying not to vomit from anxiety. I listened in fear because I never knew how bad each fight would get. Would the guns come out again? Is he going to hit her again? Will she use her favorite move and turn the car into a battering ram? Or worse, would she involve me or my brother?

I listened for the drunken statement that would send the night into chaos: "I'm taking the kids and we're leaving." This was the worst part, because it meant my drunk mother was trying to grab us and put us in her car. When my mother drove drunk, she did so at insane speeds. She'd smashed her car into telephone poles, the house we lived in, fences, and gateposts. My grandfather constantly resupplied her with vehicles, and every one of them met the same end . . . a crumpled pile of metal.

I wanted to avoid that at all costs. Unfortunately, once she decided her kids were going to be part of the fight, there was nothing my brother and I could do. Sometimes I just started running. Nowhere to go, I ran through the desert to get away. Other times, I found myself at my aunt's or sitting in the desert alone at night. Anytime I found myself alone, I daydreamed about my future. I imagined how I would change things when I finally had the chance. I wasn't even sure I'd survive till I was eighteen. Death always seemed to be right around the corner.

My brother and I were shot at by the ages of eight and ten. I was saved from taking a round to the chest by the emblem on a car trunk.

I was too young to know what was going on. All I knew was that we were again speeding down a dirt road, no seat belts, watching the dust billowing behind us. Suddenly, I saw we were not alone. A car broke through the dust, speeding down the road after us. As soon as the man driving the car made eye contact with me, a hand came out of the window. Multiple shots were fired at my brother and me as I stared at the shooter. We wouldn't know how lucky we were until we inspected the car once we were back home. One round split a hole in the roof and the other slammed directly into the trunk. Somehow, I was spared that day. (There is nothing more powerful on your journey to success than accepting the finality of life. When you fully embrace that time is limited, you focus harder, you work harder, and you are constantly racing the clock. Nothing gets put off until later; everything has an urgency to it. That man shooting at me taught me a valuable lesson: I could go at any moment. It is a surreal experience to appreciate your life at such a young age. To this day, I thank God every morning and every night. I learned early to embrace every moment and opportunity before it was all over.)

Not long after the shooting incident, my brother came to me early one morning and said he was leaving. He asked me if I wanted to go with him. "Where would we go?" I asked. He said he didn't know, but he couldn't do this any longer. I welled up with excitement at the thought of getting away. I knew very little about running away. I remember seeing a movie where the kids had sticks and handkerchiefs attached to them. I said we had to make those because it's how you run away. He agreed and we got to work. I made two peanut butter and jelly sandwiches and grabbed my favorite Ninja Turtle toy. We wrapped everything up in shirts and tied them to the sticks . . . just like the movies.

That morning we set off with a pep in our step. We talked about how our new lives would be. We allowed ourselves to imagine the possibilities of a normal childhood. Talking and walking down that road, we were free! Eight and ten years old, on a quest to start a new life. For that short while, I had never been so happy. The idea of my brother and me taking control of our situation was riveting. I had my older brother, my favorite toy, and a good meal attached to a stick. The world was going to be wide open for us. It didn't take long to realize we were walking aimlessly with nowhere to go. We agreed to start the journey at our aunt's house until we could formulate our new plan.

My imagination ran wild. I realized I could create everything I wanted in my mind. For the first time, I felt amazing simply by thinking. Just allowing myself to create a new reality made me feel free and excited. As my brother and I sat on my aunt's front porch, we tried to think of our next move. Just then, we could see a car barreling down the desert road heading in our direction. Our stomachs sank. It was too soon; we weren't ready for the experience to end. Sitting in disbelief that our aunt would snitch us out, we could make out the old brown Cadillac coming in our direction. Our journey was over. That walk was the beginning of using my imagination to escape my circumstances. Soon I would take that skill further and use it to create new realities, then I would create a plan to enact that new reality.

· · · · · · · · · · · · · · · · · · · · · · · · · · · · · ·

My time finally came when I was fifteen. I envisioned living a better life, and I came up with the idea of living with my father. I had learned my father owned a restaurant in New York. I figured having a parent in good standing with his community would be a great start. Despite having never contacted him before, I decided it was worth the risk. My mother always told us that my dad was a terrible man, and that he wanted nothing to do with us. It was time to find out for myself. I knew there was no way my mother would allow that to happen, but after all I had been through, nothing could stop me. I saw my life in a new state, with new beginnings. I crystallized the idea in my head to the point where it felt like it was already my reality. I had to escape.

So, I called my father and told him that I was ready to move to New York and start a new life. He said that first we would need to call the local police department and see what I would need to do in order not to be considered a runaway. I called the station and an officer informed me that I would need my mother to sign a note giving my father custody. That was going to be difficult, but not as difficult as getting all my things packed and out of the house without her noticing.

I started to slowly pack my belongings and hide them in the closet. I used old toys and clothes to make my room look messy so my mom would not catch on. Once I was packed and ready to go, phase one of my escape plan was complete. Phase two was going to be the most difficult part because it all had to happen at once. I had to somehow get the custody note signed, contact my father for a plane ticket, and find a ride to the airport with all my stuff.

I tried cutting out the signature portion of the note and asking my mother to sign a school note for me. She immediately lifted the sheet and read the custody letter I wrote up. She laughed and said that she would never sign custody over to my deadbeat father. I had to think of a plan B on the fly. So, I picked a fight with her. I figured I would get her so mad she would sign it just to get rid of me. After throwing about five shoes at me, she realized I wasn't going to stop. She signed the note.

Now, it was time to enact the rest of my plan before she realized how serious I was about leaving. I called my father and got the plane ticket. The problem was my flight wouldn't leave for several days. I had to think fast. I called my cousin and asked her to pick me up in the middle of the night. She agreed, and I spent three days hiding from my mother, who was actively trying to find me with the police, until my flight left. I got on the plane and never looked back.

.............................

You can't teach that kind of resiliency, creative thinking, and problem-solving. I look back on that escape plan, and I am proud of young me for being so tenacious. I have no idea if I could even do that today. It was such a bold move, but it was inspired by desperation. It was inspired by the harsh life I had lived up until that point. Poverty and trauma were shaping me into an unstoppable force. Unfortunately, it was also shaping me into an overly aggressive, anxiety-riddled troublemaker. I was becoming both the best and worst versions of myself at the same time. Soon the fork in the road would cause me to choose which version I would become.

### Addressing the Shadow

So why are we better broken? Swiss psychiatrist Carl Jung said, "No tree, it is said, can grow to heaven unless its roots reach down to hell."

Jung believed that a person cannot be complete and good without first understanding his capacity for evil. For those of us born into proverbial hells, we are acutely aware of our own capacity for evil as well as those around us. Growing up in poverty gave many the opportunity to see and do things they are not proud of. We got to know a part of ourselves Jung refers to as "the shadow," which is a dark side of our personality. It's only when the shadow is balanced with the good that we can reach our true potential.

Jung said, "Unfortunately, there can be no doubt that man is, on the whole, less good than he imagines himself or wants to be. Everyone carries a shadow, and the less it is embodied in the individual's conscious life, the blacker and denser it is. If an inferiority is conscious, one always has a chance to correct it . . . But if it is repressed and isolated from consciousness, it never gets corrected."[4]

Most who have survived abuse and neglect, or have experienced the true depths of poverty, understand that allowing our shadows to take over can offer protection and safety. When surviving in poverty, our shadows allow us to become more violent, to steal, and to commit crime without remorse. This violence gives us the ability to live in harsh environments and even thrive in those environments. This awareness of our own capacity for evil is just one reason we triumph when we learn to control it. While most struggle to acknowledge their demon's existence, the broken have been facing theirs for years.

Our aggression, when controlled and directed, becomes confidence. Our willingness to walk into danger translates into calculated risk-taking. Our ability to face our fears prevents drifting and keeps us on an achieving path. I believe Jung understood that our greatest attributes are tied to our greatest weaknesses. Only when we acknowledge the existence of both can we truly reach new heights and live up to our potential.

## Chapter 2

# TRANSITIONING FROM SURVIVING TO SUCCEEDING

"Imagine who you could be and then aim single-mindedly at that."
**—Jordan Peterson**

There are so many of us who have found success and proven that the broken are better equipped. So why are more broken people not teaching these skills? I think it is because most of us didn't realize when it was happening that we were making the transition from trauma to greatness . . . from surviving to succeeding. We were simply so happy to be moving forward and getting out of poverty that we failed to document our journeys. Thankfully, we can look toward some famous names and use their transitions as road maps. There are an abundance of celebrities, historical figures, and great leaders who come from horrible childhoods and used their trauma for greatness.

Some of these greats include Winston Churchill, Benjamin Franklin, Charlize Theron, Malcolm X, DMX, Marilyn Monroe, Curtis Jackson, Tyler Perry, Oprah Winfrey, and Will Smith. Let's take a quick look at what some of these people stated about their childhood experiences. I share these glimpses in the hopes that you realize that your own struggles are real, and that your transition from trauma to greatness is within your grasp.

> "My mother was out one night, as she loved to play bingo, and my father came home . . . mad at the world. He was drunk, as he was most of the time. He got the vacuum cleaner extension cord and trapped me in a room and beat me until the skin was coming off my back. To this day, I don't know what would make a person do something like that to a child."
> **–Tyler Perry**

Speaking to *GQ* in 2019, DMX talked about being six years old and erasing something in his mother's notebook:

"She beat two teeth out of my mouth with a broom. And I think about this today, I'm like, 'Okay, you saw me erase something in your notebook. What did you think I was trying to do? What could you have possibly thought I was trying to do?'"

Shania Twain discussing her dad's brutal abuse toward her mother to ABC News: "[It was] overwhelming for any child to never know what to expect from one day to the next. It could happen anytime. But also, you don't know if they're going to survive it."

> "I was beaten for the slightest reasons. Spilled water, a broken glass, the inability to keep quiet or still... The long-term impact of being whupped—then forced to hush and even smile about it—turned me into a world-class people pleaser for most of my life."[5]
> **—Oprah Winfrey**

In Will Smith's memoir, artistically titled *Will*, he said he had to stop looking at the present through the lens of his past. The context behind the quote was that Will was being scolded by a network executive for changing his lines in the hit show *The Fresh Prince of Bel-Air*. The executive was angrily pacing around the room. Smith felt like he was standing over him in a threatening manner, so Smith stood up and challenged him, demanding that he sit down... or else.

In that moment, it seemed perfectly logical: Smith was viewing the situation through the lens of his past. In the streets of Philadelphia, if someone takes a position like that, the fight is on. However, he wasn't in the streets of Philadelphia anymore. That executive had just had back surgery and was unable to sit down. He was pacing the office in pain. Smith had failed to change the lens he was viewing the world from. He completely misread the situation and nearly ruined a great opportunity.

This story is the perfect representation of the struggles broken people have when adapting their skills to societal success. In the streets, Smith's behavior would have been commended. He would have been praised for standing up for himself. Being viewed as strong would have increased his credibility. Yet here he was, the star of a hit TV show, and suddenly that same action is completely inappropriate. All of us broken people have had these painful transition periods.

· · · · · · · · · · · · · · · · · · · · · · · · ·

Charlize Theron was fifteen years old when her verbally abusive alcoholic father came home drunk. Her father threatened her mother with a gun. Theron's mother grabbed her own gun and started shooting back in self-defense, killing Theron's father in front of her. According to Theron, the aftermath of the incident was more traumatizing than the incident itself.

"That was my entire childhood," Theron said. "My trauma was all of that."

Theron was opening up about her childhood after winning an Oscar for her role as Aileen Wuornos in the movie *Monster*. Aileen Wuornos was a serial killer who claimed to have killed because she was raped as a prostitute.

Theron made a very revealing statement during her interview for *Insider* about the role:

"People like Aileen Wuornos that people just want to label and, like, shove under a rug, nobody wants to examine that human. Nobody wants to look at the person and say, 'But why did this happen?' I'm fascinated by the why. Because in many ways, I am here today because of the why."

Theron was able to empathize with the suffering of Wuornos and direct her own trauma into the role, essentially utilizing her trauma to become an Oscar-winning actor. Our trauma is powerful and gives us near superhuman ability. We just need to learn to harness the power!

---

Curtis Jackson, also known as 50 Cent, whose father abandoned him at birth, and whose mother, a cocaine dealer, died in a house fire. According to Curtis, someone put something in her drink and turned the gas on. He was sent to live with his grandmother at the age of twelve. He was soon arrested in school for the possession of a firearm and sent to a military-style boot camp. This is where Curtis found his love for rapping and realized he had a decision to make.

It was time for Curtis to make his transition and adapt his street education to societal success. That transition would lead to a Grammy for Best Rap Performance, BET Best New Artist, MTV Best New Artist, BET Hip Hop Award for Hustler of the Year, and a slew of other music awards. He would then go on to become a successful author, actor, producer, director, and entrepreneur. Once Curtis decided to make the transition, he became unstoppable. Everything he put his hands on seemed to turn to gold. One of my favorite books is *The 50th Law* by Curtis Jackson and Robert Greene, which documents Curtis's transition to fame and success. Nearly every tool he used to succeed was an adaptation from his time in poverty and pain.

---

So how did these celebrities transition their childhood trauma into such greatness? By learning to harness their trauma and redirect it. They decided that they were worth the effort it would take to thrive. They chose to put the work in and self-educate, relearn social behaviors, and adapt the lessons of poverty and survival. They made a choice followed by a series of daily actions that got themselves closer and closer to greatness. They honed themselves until they could harness the power of their trauma. They accepted that there were things they could not change and focused on the things they could.

## MY TRANSITION MOMENT

I earned a master's degree and became a Green Beret. I've been a police officer, a business owner, and an ultra-marathon runner, but most importantly, I have used the lessons that form this book to become a good father and a good husband. I built a home full of love and safety for my children. Like the celebrities in this chapter, I used my trauma to break the cycle of abuse. My children do not know what an empty fridge looks like; they do not have run-ins with child protective services. They know nothing but love and kindness from their parents. When I left California at the age of fifteen, nobody thought I would even graduate high school. It wasn't until my trauma nearly broke me that I decided to become more than anyone expected.

After my escape from Phelan, I found myself struggling to adapt to New York. My father and I were like roommates who barely spoke. He put me to work at his restaurant and routinely scolded me, saying I was lazy and that the staff thought I was entitled. I couldn't do anything right according to him. I couldn't sweep the floors right,

I didn't clean the mirrors right . . . nothing was good enough. I started to get the feeling he was just ashamed of me. Here he was, a prominent figure in this community, and now his son, a random, damaged teenage boy, shows up and suddenly his life isn't looking so perfect anymore. It hurt me because having come from nothing, I found myself valuing that restaurant more than anything. For the first time, I had a parent who had done something I could be proud of. I loved it there, but it was as though he didn't want me. I felt like a blemish on his clean record.

I ended up living in New York for a few years, even as the reality of surviving trauma and poverty had set in. I was living around normal people who lived normal lives. Even their small western New York town was beautiful—far from the barren desert full of wanderers, old car collectors, and drug addicts that I was used to. At some point, it became obvious that I was not like everyone else. Moving to New York made me feel just how troubled I had become during my childhood. Poverty and violence taught me many things: how to stand up for myself, how to hustle, how to think. But it also taught me things that would become detrimental to my success.

For one thing, it taught me that brutality and aggression paid. The meaner I was, the less I was targeted back in Phelan. This lesson became a curse in my new life. People outside of poverty didn't need to be so aggressive. It was unnecessary at best, and downright cruel at its worst. I felt like a feral animal that was brought into a nice home, and for the first time, I began to dislike who I was. I was uncomfortable in my own skin.

In Phelan, I had learned that to get anything in life, I had to hustle. I had learned to use my words to change people's minds. I once convinced a kid with new shoes that my old, tattered ones were better. That skill landed me my first new pair of shoes in years. I learned that a bag of candy can be purchased for a dollar, but if you sold the individual pieces in class, you could make three. I learned that if someone wants to fight, you suppress the fear and fight. I used those skills toward criminal behavior—from fights, stealing cars, to putting homemade spike strips in my enemies' driveways. I was lost when it came to applying these lessons from poverty toward a positive goal.

Then, my dad left. I made a go of it in New York, and I decided to focus on school. I found time to study and get my grades up while couch surfing with friends. It was here I met my first wife, and started to get a taste of living a normal life. But my past was never that far from me. I called it my dragon. The dragon was my short fuse, my willingness to fight instead of walking away. It was this hyperaggressive and hypercompetitive drive inside me. I called it a dragon because it would eventually burn everyone around me. This dragon was unchecked and uncontrolled. I was lost at how to use it to my advantage. I started to blame the dragon for ruining opportunities instead of working to control it.

## Fear

In poverty, failing to act could cost you everything. Every fight, every confrontation, every interaction is an opportunity for people to judge your willingness to act. People always had big words, hoping to talk their way out of a fight. Most would fail to live up to that talk and their lives would become far worse for having done so. I was always terrified of fighting; it would cause so much fear to well up inside me that my body would quiver uncontrollably. I had to learn to swallow that fear and convince my body to run toward the danger instead of away from it. If I gave in to the fear, it would get around that I was afraid. Then I would be targeted by people looking to improve their stature. I learned early to act without hesitation. If the fight was coming, it paid to be the first one swinging.

It took me decades to realize that this willingness to act was a blessing in disguise. Once the broken learn to react appropriately, their willingness to "scrap" or run toward danger will catapult them past their competition. They will find that most "successful" people in society are crippled by fear. They have dreams they never chased, goals they never began, and great ideas that never became reality. Paulo Coelho wrote in his book *The Alchemist*, "Every blessing ignored becomes a curse."[6]

The broken have learned the power of action through hardship. We have learned to be decisive and trust our guts. It is for that very reason we become leaders, achievers, and dream chasers. We do not let fear stop us from acting. We do not allow our blessings to become curses.

After high school, my new wife and I moved to California. The future seemed bright, but deep down I knew that danger lurked. My dragon was chasing me. It was only a matter of time before it caught me and ruined all the progress I had made. I was so focused on what

I might do to ruin our new life that I had never considered that she would be the one to destroy it all.

One moment changed everything. My transition period was initiated when I came home to find my wife in bed with another man. There were many possible outcomes to this event. My rage was on full display, but instead of punching the man, I punched the TV and every picture frame on the wall. Even through the anger—and after throwing a vodka bottle at the guy—I realized that I was at a crossroads. I could choose to rise above this moment and become a better man. Or I could allow it to break me and prove to my wife that she made the right decision. So, I got in the car and drove . . . and never looked back. **In this moment of transition, I realized that she cheated on the man I no longer wanted to be. This was the moment when I realized it was time to buckle down and become the man I wanted to be.**

It was a good beginning, but I had a long road yet to travel. I soon found out that wanting to be successful was not enough. I realized quickly that I was not equipped to be successful in society. My learned behaviors, mentalities, and emotional responses were getting in the way. I couldn't help but sabotage every opportunity with poor decisions.

## GETTING TO BASELINE

Throughout this book I will be referring to a term I am calling "baseline." What I mean by that is the behavioral and social skills people have when they were adequately raised and cared for. It is the baseline of success that most people start life with. For the broken, it is a fight to get to this baseline. Yet once we get there, we can start to enjoy the fruits of our trauma by using it to surpass everyone else on the way to the top.

Think of transitioning from trauma as a U-shaped curve. At the top of one side is success in poverty, street smarts, hustle, and reputation. The bottom of the U is "baseline," where most people start out their adult lives. On the right side of the U is "societal" success that we all wish to aim for—a family, great career, and dreams realized.

So, I think of the transition period as the point where broken people decide they have had enough with the lives they were born into and choose instead to follow their dreams.

Unfortunately, a lot of people who've made that decision lack the fundamental knowledge to start making progress. Without progress, it is only a matter of time before they give up on themselves. In fact, to transition our trauma from a negative influence to a positive one requires hard work, particularly in three categories: financial, behavioral, and educational.

You will have to work hard just to get to "baseline," where others started out. That was one of the most discouraging and painful processes of my life: working so hard just to fit into society as an average person. It was so difficult that I am writing this book to shorten people's transition periods. The sooner you can get to baseline, the sooner you can start using your trauma to chase your dreams. Only then will you experience the power of a rough life. Only then will you thank God every morning for the hardships you endured. It takes seeing the advantages you possess firsthand.

Financially, I was illiterate, which caused me to overspend, rack up debt, destroy my credit, and destroy numerous opportunities for advancement. Behaviorally I was incompetent, getting into fights everywhere I went and embarrassing myself by my actions. I was so uneducated—formally and informally—that I was unqualified for anything other than low-level manual labor. My life of poverty and survival left me unequipped to do anything but perpetuate the same behaviors as those around me. I was so far from baseline that just staying out of prison would be a long shot. My transition changed the course of my life, but I still had many, many lessons to learn.

· · · · · · · · · · · · · · · · · · · · · · · · ·

Since I was a kid, I wanted to be a police officer. Not just any police officer but Martin Riggs from *Lethal Weapon*. Riggs was the coolest dude I had ever seen on television. He lived in a camper on the beach with his dog. I wanted his life. His life alone on the beach was my happy place. Nobody around to create anxiety, just me and my dog living in peace. Getting to meet up with my best friend and fight crime. Life could not get much better than that. I even tried to eat a dog biscuit once to look cool like Riggs.

However, when it came time to get my act together, my first choice after realizing I wanted a better life was to become a firefighter. I was twenty-one years old, and girls loved firefighters. So, I signed up for college, got my uniform, and got to work. In California you must complete the prerequisites on your own before attending the fire academy. I started to get them done, and I was loving my new focused way of life. I could tell that success in life was far more rewarding than earning respect on the streets. I was loving the progress and feeling the wind in my sails.

Soon after, I started the last course I needed: a condensed EMT class in Big Bear Lake, California. Here, I found myself in a very familiar situation. There was a guy in my class picking a fight with one of my new friends. I offered to fight the guy on my friend's behalf, which he graciously accepted. By lunchtime, the entire class was outside circled up, and I was back in the center of it. I headbutted the guy in the nose . . . fight over.

Then things went south. The busted-nose guy's girlfriend started screaming at the sight of all the blood. This caused the instructor to come out and investigate. It didn't take long to see that he was a bleeder and that I caused it. I figured my saving grace would be that we were in EMT school. Maybe the teacher would seize the opportunity to teach some bleeding control and forget about the fight. She didn't seem to grasp the teachable moment. I was kicked out of school and back to square one.

The day after the EMT school incident, I found myself in an Army recruiter's office. I knew that I lacked discipline and structure. I accepted that I was not going to make the transition on my own and needed help. I figured that if I could conform to the military, I could correct some of my behavioral deficiencies. That was not an easy process. I found myself once again getting into fights in basic training.

One morning in particular, another soldier snapped at me when I accidentally stepped on his platoon's grappling mat. In response, I looked him in the eye and spit on the mat. The fight was on. We went at it until my drill sergeant broke us up. Why did I spit on his mat instead of apologizing? Because that's how much I embraced the mentality of my upbringing. I wasn't going to be pushed around by anybody. If there was any sign of disrespect, I fought.

That reaction became so ingrained it was almost automatic. I truly believe that my brother's and my willingness to commit violence at a young age saved us from being bullied, beaten, or molested by the sick individuals that frequented our home to date our mother. Yet, I wasn't in that environment anymore. This reaction that once saved me from predators was now my downfall.

I was being beaten into submission by my shortcomings. I started to feel like giving up was the answer. I knew how to live in my old world. I knew the rules to play by and was good at it. Suddenly, I found myself stuck between two worlds, finding success in neither of them.

You will likely find yourself desperately wanting to return to your old life. I know I did. Luckily, the Army was unwilling to let me go that easily. If they had, I may have regressed. You may not have the Army to hold you in place, forcing you to continue. **That is why I am here: to encourage you to keep going.** To give you the tools to avoid the roadblocks that nearly beat me. Sometimes just knowing you are not alone is enough. Sometimes you just need to see that someone like you made it to the other side.

I was able to keep it together long enough to get through basic training. It wasn't until I got to Airborne School that I started to realize I was different. Once real pressure was being applied, I excelled.

I'll never forget strapping a parachute to my back and standing in the door of a C-130. The C-130 is a four-engine turboprop military transport aircraft. Standing in the open door, my knees started to quiver uncontrollably. Every instinct in my body was telling me to sit down. *Don't jump. Sit down and give up. I can't jump out of this plane! What if the chute doesn't open? What if I break my ankle, a knee, my back?* My body was screaming, SIT DOWN! Then suddenly the guy in front of me started to move. It was time—my adrenaline spiked, my fear nearly taking control. I was completely overwhelmed. I looked at my hand holding the static line, the line connected from my parachute to the plane itself. All I could think was, *Am I holding it right? If I do it wrong, it could rip my hand off on exit. SHIT! My brain isn't functioning properly—what is happening?!* Suddenly it clicked, and I had an epiphany. *This is a street fight, and the enemy is that door. I must walk toward it and ignore every ounce of me that is telling me to run away. I have been here before. I have been here so many times!* And just like that, a rush of calm came over my body.

The open door and its maniacal hissing of wind quieted and became still. My body turned the noise way down. The volume inside the aircraft went from a ten to a two. I could focus again. My brain started to function not just normally, but it was firing on all cylinders. I took a step forward, looked at my right hand, and could see I was holding the line exactly how I was taught. I looked down to my left hand covering my reserve parachute handle to avoid it getting caught and pulled. I looked the jump master in the eye, and he gave me the nod and yelled, "Green light, GO!"

Suddenly I was facing the open door and it was my turn to jump. I tucked my chin to my chest and confidently stepped off that ledge and started to count. I was floating in the air with my eyes shut counting and waiting for the jerk of my chute. It happened . . . just like the instructors said it would. I floated to the ground in pure peace, knowing that I had just discovered something about myself. I just found out that my willingness to stand up, to face my fear, to fight—win or lose—could be applied to something that mattered to me.

We have all the tools for success. We just need to hone ourselves in order to use them. **We need help getting through the transition period from survival to unstoppable growth and achievement.** I am here to tell you what I wish someone had told me: You are special, you have greatness in you, and your trauma is a blessing, not a curse. You are different, and once you learn to manage your behavioral and financial habits you can achieve anything you want.

Since finding this out for myself, I have achieved some worthy goals. Once I learned to get out of my own way, I became unstoppable. I realized that my childhood was a driving force for everything I touched. I acted as though I was fearless. I was willing to lose; I was willing to fail; I would push harder than everyone else. Getting to baseline was one of the most difficult things I had ever done. But once there, the momentum kept moving me forward. I was figuring it out and it was working better than I could have possibly imagined. Success was no longer an IF; it was a WHEN.

### The Broken Should Help the Broken

The sad reality is not everyone will choose to transition. Most will continue to use their gifts to be gang members, drug dealers, and criminals. Fourteen percent of men and thirty six percent of women in the United States prison population were abused as children.[7] That equates to hundreds of thousands of men and women who were likely never told how special they truly are. They may not even realize the power they possess in the form of life lessons from their trauma. As a police officer, I witnessed broken people self-medicating in the streets day in and day out, succumbing to the pain of their pasts and choosing to escape through addiction.

These people were broken kids who wanted success in their lives, just like everyone else. We have failed to teach them how to translate their skills from the streets into societal success. We are failing to give them the tools to refocus their abundance of life lessons on good. We just ignore them as they take aim at unnoble causes. These kids could change the world if taught how to aim their efforts in a positive direction.

What if they received encouragement and education to make that transition? What if it is up to the broken to help others like us find the way? As much as I love people like Jordan B. Peterson for their clinical expertise and desire to help, they have distinct limitations; they were never there.

It is my belief that it will take the broken to convince one another that we are primed for success. That our perceived weaknesses are our greatest strengths. We can carve out the lives of our dreams with a little knowledge, focus, and effort toward a positive aim.

I was once asked in an interview if I could go back and say anything to my thirteen-year-old self, what would I say? I sat there and pictured myself at that age. I felt the rush of loneliness and a desire to be seen and cared for. I started to cry as I pictured giving my young self a hug. I just wanted a damn hug. I can't change what happened to me, but I can help someone like me carve out a better life for themselves.

Helping others is the key to fulfillment in life. There is no greater or more fulfilling experience in the world. Of course, in order to spend our lives helping others we must first achieve. We must first learn to live in a way that is worth teaching.

> "Doing things for other people is actually more rewarding than virtually anything else you can do. If you watch yourself, if you pay attention to yourself and you do something that helps someone else, and it genuinely helps them. I defy you to find another experience that is that satisfying, it is actually quite stunning."
> —Jordan B. Peterson

## Chapter 3

# RECOGNIZING AND ANALYZING YOUR TRIGGERS

"Before success comes in any man's life, he is sure to meet with much temporary defeat, and, perhaps, some failure. When defeat overtakes a man, the easiest and most logical thing to do is to quit. That is exactly what the majority of men do."
**—Napoleon Hill**

The transition into societal success is difficult. There is no easy path or quick fix. This is a long journey that requires patience, self-reflection, forgiveness, and, most importantly, a commitment to the person you wish to become.

In the beginning of your journey, there will be a lot of self-reflection to determine your triggers. This is an important step; you cannot change yourself or your environment if you are clueless to your triggers.

## WHAT TRIGGERS YOU?

What issues do you face when doing "normal" things? What causes you anxiety, turmoil, and strife?

It took me a long time to realize the scope of my triggers. That was an uncomfortable period of my life. It seemed like every time I turned around, I found another issue. I found another thing that I needed to work on to get to baseline. Things kept adding to the list, but nothing was coming off. I became overwhelmed with the number of issues I had.

Once I started to look hard at myself, I became depressed with just how bad off I was. It felt like I was too far gone. The idea of becoming "normal" seemed like a hopeless dream.

Most people don't need to do breathing exercises before going to the grocery store. For the broken, going to the store means crowds, driving, anxiety, and stress. Most people have no issues with crowds; they flow in and out like nothing is amiss.

I spent most of my time trying to visualize where everything is in the store so I could get in and out before I lost my cool. Before the inevitable encounters took place, shoulder bumps, awkward standoffs, oblivious shoppers forcing me to move. These things send me into a tailspin of anxiety and frustration. I have left my items in the shopping cart and walked out on numerous occasions after interactions like these.

Regardless of how many issues you find, it is important to identify them. Do not be afraid of the increasing list you develop. **You do not have to address all your issues at once, nor should you even try. The first step is to simply identify them.**

Every time you feel anxiety, write it down. (More on this in the "Journaling" chapter.) Every time you feel anger, write it down. Look for the common themes to these emotional responses. Are you finding that certain people trigger you? Or is it situational? The more data you can compile, the easier the next phase will be.

## UNCOVERING TRIGGERS

As I journeyed to uncover my triggers, I found that two indicators worked best for me: evaluating my actions after the fact and the reactions of those who love me.

**My gut never lied and never cared about my feelings or desires.** I either felt good or felt bad about my actions. Someone cuts me off, and I ignore them . . . I feel good. Someone cuts me off, my blood boils, and I try to run them off the road . . . I become overwhelmed with guilt and self-disappointment.

I wanted more than anything to stop messing up. Every ounce of me desired to feel in control. I was so tired of walking around feeling like a ticking time bomb.

Often, we can find triggers by focusing on our loved ones. Their reactions to our behaviors are amazing indicators. For more than a decade, my North Star—my second indicator—in these situations has been my wife, Pam. Pam is from Peru and grew up in true poverty until she was ten. She lived with her grandparents in Peru because her parents were split, and her mother went to the United States to try and create a new life. My wife tells me stories of watching her grandmother sweep the rain out of the house because portions of their home had no ceiling. Her grandfather, a seamster, used to walk to the market to get the day's portion of food. Despite having so little, all she remembers is the love her grandparents showered her with.

Her mother decided it was time to bring her to the States when she was ten. Her mother by this point was working two jobs and was rarely home. Pam was thrown into school not speaking a word of English. She would hide in bathroom stalls and cry, wishing she could go back to Peru. She rarely talks about the trials of her uprooted life, but when she does it breaks my heart.

I have no doubt that her struggles made her who she is today. She is in fact better broken in every way. Her childhood created in her an intense level of empathy and understanding for others. For the last decade she has used that empathy and understanding to help me stay focused on my goals. She has warned me when my ego starts to take over—just as it did when I joined Special Forces, and it was Pam who forced me to face my actions. **Her reactions to my actions indicated that I was missing the mark.** She was not impressed by barfights and displays of machismo. Worse, she was clearly disappointed by them. Her disappointment, paired with my own, was more than enough to paint a clear picture of what I needed to work on.

## THE WRONG INDICATORS OF SUCCESS

One of the mistakes I made was using the wrong indicators to evaluate my growth. One of the indicators I tried to use was career success. If

I was succeeding at work, I must be doing something right. My time on the Special Forces Operational Detachment Alpha (ODA) taught me that was the wrong answer.

One day, my team was conducting a training event at the shooting range. We started competing to see who could shoot down the most targets in the shortest amount of time. One of my teammates started talking trash about how he was beating me. This was particularly embarrassing for me because I was one of the team's weapons sergeants. Weapons sergeants are responsible for maintaining and operating every weapon system used by the detachment along with weapons used by our allies. Part of that responsibility is being proficient so you can teach proficiency to host nation forces.

My teammate got under my skin, and I told him that if he didn't stop, I was going to hurt him. One of the senior guys on the team overheard my threat and wanted to watch the two new guys duke it out. So he called over the rest of our team and they circled around us. Here was my chance to be my old self and use it to thrive in my new environment. Looking back on the situation, I wish I would have refused to fight my teammate. I wish I would have resisted the temptation to fall backwards and be a clown for their entertainment. Instead, I saw a chance to do what I wanted to do, what I was comfortable doing. In that moment, I gave up on my goal to change, to be better. I charged my teammate and we fought.

The instance was celebrated by my team. I could tell that they were impressed by my willingness to fight. I started to find myself picking fights at bars and instigating confrontations. I was trying to earn their respect like I did in the streets growing up. I nearly got arrested after a barfight where I tried to smash a guy with a barstool. I was a Green Beret; I was supposed to be past this behavior. Instead,

I found an opportunity to make it work in my interest. That is not winning, that is not transitioning; that was using my environment as an excuse. My gut was telling me to stop. I knew what I was doing was wrong.

. . . . . . . . . . . . . . . . . . . . . . . . . . . . .

**Reverting to old behavior will happen; however, finding ways to make your old behavior work is not success.** You need to acknowledge that growth is about being the person you wish to be, not just obtaining a goal.

**My goal was to be accepted and respected by my teammates. I put that goal above my transition to success. I could have obtained that same goal without compromising my morals and personal objectives.** Yet, in the moment, I chose to do what came easier to me. I chose to fight with my fists instead of putting in the work. I wanted instant results; I didn't want to be patient and prove myself over time. I wanted to achieve my goal now, and that caused me to take shortcuts.

That instance taught me that career success was not a good indicator. I needed true personal growth; I needed to feel good about my actions; I needed to listen to my gut. Ernest Hemingway put it simply: "So far, about morals, I know only that what is moral is what you feel good after and what is immoral is what you feel bad after."

I have spent enough time feeling bad about my actions and feeling guilt over my road rage, overreactions, and temper. I was done feeling bad. The best way I have learned to stop feeling bad is by prioritizing **morals over career success**. When we do that, we feel good about ourselves and our actions, which in turn inspires us to push harder and be even better.

## NEW GAME, NEW RULES

> "Ego is the enemy of what you want and of what you have: Of mastering a craft. Of real creative insight. Of working well with others. Of building loyalty and support. Of longevity. Of repeating and retaining your success. It repulses advantages and opportunities. It's a magnet for enemies and errors. It is Scylla and Charybdis."
> **–Ryan Holiday**

Our egos are responsible for a large portion of our desire to revert to our old lives. As we start to transition out of poverty, we are leaving behind the only success we've known. We are having to learn a new game with new rules. Imagine showing up to a college soccer game and saying, *I am here to play for the first time!* You get in there, no shin guards, no cleats, no idea what's going on. You get destroyed, your ego gets crushed, and you want to go back and play the game you know. At least then you'll know the rules; you'll have a chance. This is how the transition will feel. Be aware and continue to play despite your failures. It gets better.

**Your process of finding your triggers will never really end—but once you have a solid list to draw on, it's time to do something about them.** If you are like me, the list is far longer than you hoped it would be. My list was downright overwhelming.

At first, I tried to tackle everything on my list at once. I was just going to stop and do better. A cold turkey quitting of all things negative. I was going to be slow to anger, and quick to forgiveness. Just rub my earlobes and *woosah* my way through it like Marcus from *Bad Boys*. This approach backfired and caused me to react even more aggressively and erratically than before. Attempting to suppress my triggers, I just caused them to build up for a bigger explosion.

I started to learn that during the transition into success my mental health became increasingly fragile. As I spent more and more time focusing on my issues, the glaring reality of my shortcomings started to weigh on me. I desperately needed a win; I needed to see progress to overcome the feeling of hopelessness. However, the cold turkey approach was making things far worse.

The cold turkey approach became a vicious cycle of mistake, awareness, reflection, commitment to change, repeat mistake. Each time I made the same mistake, I would fall apart. I would begin berating myself in the hopes that I would "learn my lesson." I hoped that self-deprecation would prevent future failures. All I was doing was beating myself into oblivion and seeing no progress. I was still anxious. I was still angry. I still couldn't control my impulsive behavior.

Finally, I decided to try something different. I acknowledged that I could not focus on all my triggers at once. I needed a different approach, something that would allow me to see and feel progress.

Around that time, the talk of a family Disney World trip started coming up. My daughter was ten years old and had been talking about going since she learned to speak. *Frozen* was a movie that played on an endless loop in our home. We took her to the show Disney on Ice, and she wore an Elsa dress so often we had to buy multiple dresses to wash them. This trip was going to be one of the top things she'd ever wanted.

Then the reality set in that my wife was having to plan the trip without me. We both knew that Disney World was a magical place for kids but an absolute nightmare for people with issues. Thousands of people crammed into small spaces, overpriced everything, the Florida heat sending temperatures and tempers through the roof. I had a choice to make: miss seeing my daughter finally get her dream trip, or get my act together and fast.

This deadline forced me to try something new. I knew that my energy was limited, and that I could only focus on so much and still be effective. **So, I decided to prioritize my triggers.** I created a list of them and ranked them from high priority to low priority, depending on how they affected my life.

Missing Disney World with my family was at the very top of that list. At the bottom of my list were things like anxiety in grocery stores and restaurants. By doing this, I could focus my energy on preparing for the Disney trip. This would allow me to go on the trip and enjoy the time with my family. I accepted that the more energy I spent on the Disney trip meant less energy spent on things farther down the list.

I spent weeks visualizing the crowds of people. I visualized getting bumped into, people being rude, getting ignored, having to constantly watch my kids so they didn't get lost or kidnapped. I was using my energy resources to visualize the trip and acclimate myself to the stress. It felt like I was getting controlled repetitions in—similar to mental reps we utilized in training for Special Forces and the police department.

This approach is utilized by some of the most elite performers on the planet. Consider this research conducted by psychologists Taylor, Pham, Rivkin, and Armor in 1998: "Mental simulation provides a window on the future by enabling people to envision possibilities and develop plans for bringing those possibilities about . . . mental simulation of the process for reaching a goal or of the dynamics of an unfolding stressful event produced progress in achieving those goals or resolving those events."[8]

Using this technique allowed me to anticipate emotional responses to negative interactions. This helped me to preplan appropriate reactions. I started to develop alternative narratives for those instances. For example, if someone bumps into me, it is more likely that they are trying to avoid bumping into someone else. If they are rude, maybe they are just overwhelmed by the environment.

Having these preplanned reactions rehearsed in my mind would allow me to quickly recover from a negative interaction. Instead of my mind instantly jumping to *this person is trying to instigate me—they are inconsiderate; I should say something*, my mind could pull the preplanned empathetic responses instead. *This person was trying to watch out for their kids. They were avoiding so many people; it was an accident*. This empathetic outlook almost completely neutralized the anxiety associated with crowds and personal space.

When the trip finally came, I was ready. To the shock of my wife and myself, it went better than I imagined. Everyone was far more respectful than I prepared for. They seemed to move out of my way like a choreographed routine. I didn't get bumped into once, despite the park being absolutely packed. I had built myself up mentally to handle more than reality had in store for me.

My mental preparation for this event changed my behavior toward others. I realized that my anxiety perpetuates negativity. Getting those negative emotional responses under control changed the way people around me treated me. The trip was an absolute success, and one I almost had to miss.

When we focus our energy correctly, we can think our way through almost any trigger. Unfortunately, the energy required to do so is limited. **It is imperative that you accept those limitations in order to use the energy wisely by prioritizing your triggers and focusing on the ones that are impacting your life the most.** You will see something that we all need to see: progress. If you take the cold turkey or shotgun blast approach to your triggers, not only will you fail to control them, but they will start to gain even more control over you.

## AVOIDING YOUR TRIGGERS

Now that you have identified your triggers, prioritized them, and analyzed them to determine which ones are high priority, it's time to look at avoiding low-priority triggers!

I found that by changing my environment, I could avoid a lot of low-priority triggers. Simply avoiding them reduced my level of stress and anxiety drastically. This freed up more energy, energy that I redirected toward higher-priority triggers. This had a compounding effect, and I started to see results at a much higher rate.

Avoidance can be a very powerful tool. As a police officer, we were taught a concept called Crime Prevention Through Environmental Design (CPTED). The idea is that we can avoid crime by manipulating our environment. The five principles of CPTED are physical security, surveillance, movement control, management and maintenance, and defensible space. As a rookie I thought the idea of CPTED was a cop-out. How are shrubs going to prevent crime? I just pictured some police chief hopelessly convinced the safety of his city rested on flowerpots and thorn vines.

Yet the more I thought about it, the more it made sense. If I were to use my Special Forces experience to protect a high value target (HVT), the first thing I would do is check the environment. Is there adequate lighting to prevent ease of undetected movement? Is there surveillance? Can we create natural serpentine barriers with landscaping?

Why would we not apply this same approach to our own lives? We can utilize the concept of CPTED to avoid triggers. **We can manipulate our environment for maximum safety of our mental health.**

This will require some imagination and flexibility on your part. It will not always be an easy thing to do. However, the more successful you become, the easier it will be to change your environment.

For example, I couldn't imagine using rideshare apps to avoid driving when I was poor. I could barely afford gas, let alone pay someone to haul me around. Now I use rideshare apps whenever possible. Why? Driving has always been a trigger for me. So, I avoid it at all costs, opting to spend the money on Uber or Lyft. Side note: My willingness to rideshare has allowed my family to operate with one vehicle, saving us insurance and another car payment. From a cost perspective, there are substantial savings.

Another lower-priority trigger that I have opted to avoid is grocery shopping. Rather than going to the store and dealing with rude people who have zero spatial awareness, I choose instead to have my groceries delivered for a $10.00 delivery fee. Not only is $10.00 worth every penny in order to avoid grocery shopping, but we also save on average $50.00 a week shopping online. Shopping in the store causes us to grab far more unexpected and unneeded items.

One of the most important trigger-avoiding moves my wife and I made was choosing the right neighborhood. My wife and I put a ton of thought into what neighborhood we would live in. We wanted something gated, something that felt safe. We knew that we would spend more and get less just to have that feeling of comfort and safety. However, the number of low-priority triggers that are avoided by a good neighborhood with good schools is immense.

Not every avoidance technique needs to cost money. Changing your driving route to and from work could help avoid certain highways where road rage incidents are common. Bringing a lunch to work or eating in your car could help avoid negative coworkers. Not watching the news in the morning, avoiding social media, or muting certain contacts in your phone are all environmental controls to protect your mental health. Go through your low-priority list and get creative in finding ways to avoid those triggers. In jiu-jitsu it is often said, "If you can't move your opponent, move yourself." In this way, you're using two approaches to achieve the same goal. With time, those low-priority triggers will be the only ones left on your list, and you can choose to face and overcome them. Until then, use that energy to overcome the triggers that are impacting your self-esteem, hurting relationships, or preventing you from achieving your goals.

## Broken and Wanting to Be Seen

Not too long ago, I was sitting with a friend, and we started to talk about trauma. My friend's childhood was immensely difficult. Her father has a very twisted reality of Indian culture and how women should be treated. He is a cruel man and wreaked havoc on her emotional well-being.

My friend is an amazingly successful ER doctor at a major hospital. While we were talking, she told me the first thing she wanted to be when she grew up was an actor. That struck me instantly. It was the same for me. I struggled with why I wished for that career for decades. I always wanted to know what drew my attention toward that life. Why did I want to be an actor so desperately when I was young?

I asked her why she thought that was, why two broken people chose acting, of all things. I wasn't expecting her reply.

My friend looked at me and said, "Nobody is more seen than an actor."

As soon as she said this, a wave of emotion overtook me. The answer I had been seeking was just casually dropped in my lap. *I was desperate to be seen.* Being an actor would put me on the biggest stage on the planet. It would force my dad to see me; it would force everyone to know who I am. It would force them to see there was something special about me.

Both my friend and I moved on from our acting dreams. She was accepted into a prestigious medical school, and I joined the military to find structure. What we learned along the way was that we didn't need to be seen by others. We just needed to see and appreciate ourselves. We knew our potential; we knew that trauma had formed us into something different, and now it was time to put our beliefs into action. It was time to prove that we were better broken.

## Chapter 4

# ELIMINATE NEGATIVITY

*"I will eliminate hatred, envy, jealousy, selfishness, and cynicism by developing love for all humanity, because I know that a negative attitude toward others can never bring me success. I will cause others to believe in me, because I will believe in them, and in myself."*
**–Napoleon Hill**

During the transition to success, you will be more vulnerable than ever. Your constant self-analysis will leave you with little energy to block out negativity. **It is vital that you create a safe environment void of unnecessary drama and negativity.**

Negativity comes in many forms, and as it turns out, our brains are hardwired to focus on it. Researchers Paul Rozin and Edward Royzman coined the term "negativity bias," which is a principle that states that in most situations, "negative events are more salient, potent, dominant in combinations, and generally efficacious than positive events."[9]

And if you're wondering why we choose to focus on negativity despite the potential side effects, Rozin and Royzman found four elements that explain why the negativity bias manifests:

1. "Negative potency" suggests that despite the severity of two events being equal in terms of emotionality or magnitude, the negative event will have a greater emotional impact or salience.
2. As we get closer to a negative event, our fears and anxieties heighten at a greater rate, compared to good feelings as we get closer to a positive event.
3. Negativity dominance suggests that we overshadow entire events and/or people based on the negative rather than the positive. The example given in their research is that losing $100 is worse than winning $100 is good; therefore the potency of negativity will likely outweigh the overall experience.
4. Negative differentiation is the idea that since negative events are typically more complicated than positive ones, the negative events require more cognitive resources to overcome, causing them to be more impactful.[10]

But what concerns me the most about negativity comes from Dr. Daniel Amen, who believes that negative thinking rewires our neural networks and strengthens pathways in the brain to make us more likely to see the glass as half-empty. "Our brain-imaging work shows that *feeling bad further affects the brain, reducing activity in an area involved with self-control, judgment, and planning. This increases the odds of making bad decisions, which leads to more Automatic Negative*

*Thoughts (ANTs), which makes you feel worse. It's a downward spiral that can take a serious toll on your well-being.*"[11] (Italics are mine.)

Does this sound familiar? Is this not the cycle of the broken working toward self-improvement? Attempting to make a change only to give in to a trigger and feel overwhelmed with guilt, further reducing our ability to make better decisions? Our trauma has caused deep-rooted negativity neuropathways in our brains. Therefore, the actions we take to protect ourselves and correct those neuropathways toward positivity is crucial.

So, what does this mean and what does it have to do with our personal transition into success? It is important to understand the severity of negativity as well as the source of it. By acknowledging our propensity for negativity, we can create boundaries and protect ourselves from it. And protecting ourselves from negativity is crucial.

By having a positive outlook regarding my future, I have not only reduced my level of stress and anxiety, but I am also excited about what is to come. I have taken advantage of neural plasticity to strengthen my neural pathways and redirect them toward positivity. (Neural plasticity is the ability of the nervous system to change in response to extrinsic or intrinsic stimuli.)

## WHERE NEGATIVITY COMES FROM

What negativity do we need to exclude from our lives? Well, that is entirely up to you. I suggest keeping a journal handy and writing things down when they upset you. You can make a note in your phone, send an email to yourself, make a sticky note. Negativity needs to be paid attention to. Is it another person? Does your stomach sink when you get a text or a call from an individual? That is a clue. The following are ways that I have chosen to avoid negativity in my life. By doing so, my brain stays in a positive state that allows me to focus on my future and my goals.

## Politics and the News

Let's focus on a very common negative influence and how we can start limiting it. There is no question that our negativity bias is being utilized by the news. Politics, especially, has become a trigger for nearly everyone, whether they have broken pasts or not. As a country, we love to get riled up about politics. We love to complain and throw our opinions out there like we are making a difference.

So, I'm just going to say it: You're not changing anyone's mind. There is no tweet, repost, or hashtag on the planet that is going to convert anyone. Getting upset about politics and politicians is a giant waste of your mental energy. That energy can be focused on transitioning into success and living the life you deserve. You did not survive abuse, torment, and poverty to spend your adult life pissed off about things you can't control. I know I didn't. Let the anger of politics be argued by those who have nothing better to do. **We have a life to live.** We have personal changes to make and abilities to take advantage of. When it is time to vote, you can be the first in line, but until that day, you need to let politics go and avoid it at all costs.

Since I gave up paying attention to politics and the news, my mental health has improved tenfold. Even during the pandemic. (Scratch that . . . especially during the pandemic!) I cut it all off and never looked back. The fearmongering was so out of control that I could feel my chest tightening every time I listened. The media couldn't care less if they destroyed your life through panic and hysteria. You could have a panic attack, heart attack, or start hitting the bottle or abuse drugs as a result, *just as long as you click*. I refuse to allow them to destroy my mental health over clicks, views, and likes. I refuse to allow them to use my negativity bias for a profit.

## Social Media

Social media was a different kind of stress for me. It was less about negativity and more about feeling insecure about my accomplishments. I was following some of the most successful people I knew: Evan Hafer, founder of Black Rifle Coffee; Nick Bare, founder of Bare Performance Nutrition; and Bedros Keuilian, founder of Fit Body Boot Camp. And honestly, it was making me feel more insecure than ever. These guys are not only great humans, but they have also personally helped me become a better entrepreneur. I have no doubt that I will reach their level of success one day; however, watching their success unfold through social media was bringing me down.

Think about how many people you follow on social media: hundreds, if not thousands. Out of hundreds of people, at least a handful are doing something big at every moment. So, it gives us this feeling that, at any given moment, somebody is making a big move, going on vacation, getting promoted. How do you stack up to that? Can you compete with hundreds of people? Of course not, but social media once again is about clicks, views, and likes. They couldn't care less that they are making you feel inferior—just stay on the app.

I decided to unfollow everyone on Instagram besides my company, my wife, and my business partners. It was surreal how hard it was to do that. I was nervous that they would take it as a slight against them. More so, I was nervous I was going to miss out on something. Social media was messing me up mentally in ways I didn't even realize.

Since then, I spend almost no time on the app, and I feel amazing. Getting off social media allowed me to stop feeling like I am behind in the business world and start focusing on how far I have come. Even if you own a company and rely on social media for marketing, you can post it and ghost it. You don't need to read every comment; you don't need to engage with every person. You need to protect your mental health first and foremost. If you are honest with your followers as to why you don't engage as often, they will likely understand and respect your willingness to have boundaries. I have found that on my YouTube channel, The FNG Academy, my followers respect my openness about my insecurities and shortcomings. As a channel dedicated to helping people get selected for Special Operations, it is important that it conveys to my viewers that Green Berets struggle just like everyone else.

Some people may not have issues with social media; however, I know that my mental health is vulnerable and needs to be protected. I am proud of my friends and their successes; I genuinely want them to achieve their dreams. I now choose to support my friends through prayers instead of likes and comments. Doing so has often caused me to think about them and reach out, strengthening our bonds. Likes and hearts are so diluted and require no thought or effort. If you truly care about someone, send them a prayer or positive wishes. If you haven't talked in a while, send a text or give them a call.

## Family

I wish eliminating negativity was as easy as unfollowing people and not listening to the news. Unfortunately, sometimes the most negative things in our lives are our family members.

I knew from an early age that I wanted to get as far away from my mother as possible. To this day she is not involved in my life. I wish I had a positive story of redemption and renewed relationships, but that just isn't the case. My mother has never met either of her granddaughters because of it.

I haven't talked to my father in years, either. Again, it is for the best. We never developed a lasting bond, likely the result of not meeting until I was a teenager. It took me a long time to accept that I don't have a relationship with either of my parents.

I learned quickly that I could not change who my parents were. However, I could change myself and become the parent I wished they had been. So, that is exactly what I have done. I have taken every ounce of energy from their absence and focused it on being a better father. It has been far more rewarding to be a good father than to have one.

In other words, we need to take responsibility for our lives. We are no longer children or victims. The world continues to spin, and we have grown up. It's time to focus on the next generation. We were abused, so don't let it happen to them. We had absentee fathers and abusive mothers—don't be that to them. It is not about us anymore, it is about them, and we need to break the cycles of abuse and create new patterns. Our parents were not successful, so we will be. We will not live in poverty; we will learn to manage money and control our behavior. We will right their wrongs.

I know firsthand that eliminating or reducing contact with negative family members can be extremely difficult. Regardless of how negative they are in your life, there is still a tie that is hard to cut. I believe that stems from growing up in poverty. When you live in poverty, you always live on the brink of disaster. You are always one paycheck away from debt collectors, not paying your bills, or not eating.

When you live without any emergency reserves, the people around you become that reserve. You start to see each other as a resource when there is not enough. This creates a communal living situation where everyone is interdependent because nobody is thriving.

You will find that when you set boundaries and stick to them, your family will come to you less and less. They will see that you are no longer a resource or part of their communal living. This can be a scary transition because that means you no longer have *them* as a resource. Yet it is vital to create distance from those who bring negativity into your life. Soon they will quit trying to pull you back in, and you can live free from their drama.

You are not a bad person for creating distance from negative family members. If they truly want to be part of your life, they will change their negative ways and work to bring positivity and value to you. The best family is the one you choose—the ones who try to be involved and contribute to you just as much as you contribute to them. Family is not something we are born into and are required to deal with no matter what. Blood does not make family; family is a person or persons you choose to love because that love is reciprocated.

## Your Inner Circle

After turning my back on family members who created nothing but negativity for me, I was able to start creating my inner circle. I hadn't realized it at the time, but this would be one of the most important things I had ever done. I had cut ties with the negative people in my life, and it felt amazing. Now I was going to take it a step further and start adding positive influences.

When you transition into success, you will be working nonstop. You will be working on self-improvement, career advancement, and physical and mental health. You will be in a constant state of pushing for more knowledge, more abilities, and getting better incrementally every day. This nonstop work can get tiresome, and you will find yourself needing motivation and support.

That is where your inner circle comes in. If you choose to keep people around you who are goal-oriented, focused, and driven, they will propel you forward. They will keep you on track because their own drive will motivate you to be better. I have made hundreds of acquaintances in my life. I have called many people friends. However, there have only been a handful of people who truly make me feel better about who I am as a person. When I am feeling down or worn out, I look to them to lift me back up. They are always adding value to my life, and I try hard to add value to theirs. They are my family, some by blood, but most by choice.

## ROOT IT OUT!

This road is hard. We need all the advantages we can get. Negativity will hold us back and prevent us from living up to our potential. So, family or not, negative people need to go. The news needs to be shut off, especially if it is causing you anxiety or getting you fired up. Leave the politics to politicians, and don't let them force you into a fight on their behalf. Don't fall for it. Be better than that. Choose to put your mental health first.

The answer to negativity is not just removing it; it should be replaced. Negative people can be replaced with positive ones.

Negative information can be replaced with positive information. I don't wake up and turn on the news. I wake up and listen to an audiobook or a podcast from someone I admire. What goes into my head is positive; this gives me a more hopeful outlook on my future, and I work harder to obtain it.

From here on out, you need to discover who and what brings negativity into your life. Take notes and keep documentation. If your phone rings and your stomach sinks, that is a problem. If you get a text message and your palms start sweating, that is a problem. If every time someone calls you, it is to talk bad about other people or spew negativity, that is a problem. If the news causes you to curse at the television and post hateful memes on Instagram, that is a problem.

Once you have identified the negativity, you can get beyond it. People are tricky. Some will get the point when you stop contacting them. Others will need to be told of your plan to focus on yourself. However, you can expect resistance here.

Don't forget that you are hardwired for negativity, so at times you may miss the phone calls bashing others. You may miss the fired-up feeling of politics and hate-mongering. You may feel drawn toward the comment section of controversial topics. However, replacing that negativity with positivity will be key.

When someone who brings negativity into your life calls, I suggest you don't answer. Instead, start developing a list of positive people who motivate you to do better. Check in with people who lift your spirits and who are driven. Find out what they are doing, and feed off their energy. Support them as much as you can. Live by the idea that to succeed you must help others.

When we focus on achieving and helping others do the same, we will have little room for negativity. Our lives become so full of hope and excitement toward the future that negative thoughts can't dwell in our minds. Anxiety lessens, and soon, triggers start to fade and become easier to manage. Never forget what Uncle Ben said in Spider-Man: "With great power comes great responsibility."

We are all equipped with great power. We weren't bit by radioactive spiders; instead we earned our powers through surviving hardship and abuse. The things that we've endured created a hunger inside of us. That hunger is partnered with unparalleled life experience. We are better broken, because being broken has made us unique, driven, and focused. We know our shadows, as Jung would put it. We have faced darkness that would bring most to their knees. Yet here we are, focusing on ourselves and not blaming others or asking why. If that isn't the recipe for a superhero, then I don't know what is.

## Chapter 5

# REJECTION IS OKAY

"Our visions are the world we imagine, the tangible results of what the world would look like if we spent every day in pursuit of our WHY."
**–Simon Sinek**

Growing up with a traumatic childhood has a lot of second- and third-order effects. One of those effects can often be the fear of rejection. We choose to leave poverty behind to get away from rejection. However, professional rejection is not the same; it is not personal. Rejection in poverty could mean you don't eat or are left unprotected and vulnerable. In the professional world, it is a chance to hone yourself and your goals. If you fail to gain control of your fears of rejection, you may struggle to take risks and pursue a meaningful life.

It was just as Robert Greene described in his book *The 50th Law*: "In impoverished environments, people's sense of who they are and what they deserve is continually under attack. People from the outside tend to judge them for where they come from as violent, dangerous, or untrustworthy, as if the accident of where they were born determines who they are. They tend to internalize many of these judgements and perhaps deep inside feel that they don't deserve much of what is considered good in this world."[12]

## THE SIDE EFFECTS OF REJECTION

Some of the side effects that lasted well into my adult life were automatic negative thoughts and not feeling good enough. The automatic negative thoughts are still something I struggle with. I found that talking with people I trust is imperative before making decisions. As soon as someone doesn't write me back, or responds in a questionable manner, I jump to the worst conclusions possible. I assume I angered them or did something wrong. I assume they had ill intentions or they were using me.

## TAKE A PAUSE

This mindset can be disastrous in professional social environments. If you suffer from automatic negative thoughts, it is vital that you acknowledge them and learn to take a tactical pause. This will allow you to avoid acting on those thoughts and instead seek counsel from your inner circle. I call someone from my inner circle regularly to seek advice. It usually starts with me claiming, "I pissed off this person and our working relationship is likely over," and ends with,

"You're right . . . they probably got busy and didn't have time to write me back."

The difference between automatic responses from myself and my peers is drastic. I find it incredible how they just assume everything is fine and choose not to worry about it. Meanwhile, I work myself into a frenzy trying to figure out what I did wrong. Then, inevitably, the truth comes out, and 99 percent of the time, my inner circle was right and I was overreacting.

It can be heartbreaking at times to come to terms with the neurological changes that took place because of our trauma.

## STOP REJECTING YOURSELF

For many years, I struggled with a feeling of not being good enough. To combat this feeling of inadequacy, I did the opposite of what I wanted to do. Instead of avoiding failure and rejection, I ran toward it. I figured that if I faced the big, scary monster, I could defeat it. I used ambition, drive, and determination as a way of coping with my fear. Yet with every achievement, I felt worse.

It wasn't until I dug into my past and realized that my trauma made me better that I started to become proud of who I am. You will never stop fearing rejection until you stop rejecting yourself. Once you have embraced yourself, nobody can reject you ever again. If you have already given yourself permission to be great, you don't need anyone else to do it for you. As children we can be rejected or thrown away by our parents, guardians, or peers. As adults, the only person who determines if we are good enough is us.

## REJECTION FOR SUCCESS

When I stopped rejecting myself, my trauma became a badge of honor instead of an ugly scar. That was a turning point in my willingness to allow real rejection from the outside world. I knew that in order to be successful, rejection was a necessary part of the process. I finally became ready to embrace that rejection and use it as a tool.

I discovered that rejection now (as an adult) is not the same as rejection then. As a kid, rejection was personal. It was parents and family members choosing themselves over me. It was being avoided by others for being poor and perceived as violent or untrustworthy.

Rejection today is a powerful tool that can be utilized for growth. I have come to realize that rejection in the world of success is not a personal attack. It is instead a chance for you to see areas of improvement.

Rejection in this world means something isn't working *yet*. That is an opportunity for you to find out why and work on it. For example, when I started my company, The FNG Academy, I knew that at some point I wanted to produce a line of energy shots called "Buck Shot!" (My nickname is Buck.) The bottle would have a photo of me holding a shotgun like Elmer Fudd. Get it? "Buck Shot!" Okay . . . it sounds stupid when I write it down, but you get the idea.

So, because I am impulsive, I instantly shot my friend a text. He owns a nutrition company, so if anyone could help me make Buck Shot! a reality it was him. He responded with a voice text, and it was the most beautifully crafted "no" I have ever heard. That voice message taught me a lot about the game of business and rejection. He broke down the ways I would need to improve on my end in order to make a partnership like that successful for everyone.

I immediately started taking notes from the message. That "rejection" was lined with golden nuggets on how to improve my reach and run a more efficient business. Once my business was at the right level, I would have bargaining power to make these ideas come to life. Within that "no" were more teachable moments than any yes could offer.

Rejection in the professional world can come in many forms. You were passed up for a promotion, not selected for Special Forces, or denied a business opportunity. It is important that you accept those moments for what they are: massive growth opportunities. The only way those moments hurt your growth is if you allow them to stop forward progression. I have had rejections bring me to physical illness and tears. Those moments were so painful, and I felt like moving forward was no longer an option. Yet by pushing through, I am now able to use those moments to teach others. I was gifted the most knowledge from the most painful rejections.

A teachable moment that stings will stick with us. The sting forces us to pay attention. Now that we are paying full attention, we can start mining the experience for improvements. This allows us to walk away from the professional rejection better than we were before. This approach puts us in a constant state of winning. As the saying goes, *we are either winning or learning*.

Winning feels good, but learning gets us closer to our ideal version of ourselves. For the broken, growth is more valuable than a single win. We don't want to win once; we want to learn the formula so we can win infinitely. Once we have proven that the formula is effective, we can focus on our true "why," which for me is to teach . . . to show kids living in poverty that their trauma has made them unstoppable. To give them hope.

## Chapter 6

# FORGIVENESS IS KEY

*"Do as the heavens have done, forget your evil;*
*With them forgive yourself."*
**–William Shakespeare**

As broken people we must accept that our traumatic pasts will continue to affect us. We must learn to forgive ourselves for making mistakes in order to move forward. Broken people are often their own worst critics. We expect a lot from ourselves because we have survived so much. We have overcome such great obstacles just by making it to this point and we understand that we are capable and powerful. However, we will stumble, nobody is perfect, and the lack of forgiveness for self and others will derail our future.

You are setting out on a journey to discover your greatness and use it to live the life of your dreams. Because you are broken, you started the journey in a deficit. Due to no fault of your own, you lack certain skills to achieve that dream. You have embraced your deficit and decided to correct it through education and self-exploration. This journey will have you in a near constant state of self-evaluation in order to find your triggers, to determine their root cause, and to work toward controlling them.

If you are like me, one of your biggest struggles is impulsive actions that cause shame and regret. Have you ever acted out impulsively and felt physically sick from your own behavior? Have you ever acted like a complete jerk for no reason? Have you ever acted out of such intense anger that, after the incident, you felt like you were in a fog? As though you were someone else watching from a distance?

One day, I was driving in the car with my wife and my oldest daughter. A man cut me off and slammed on the brakes. He thought I was driving too slowly. This act sent me into a rage. I drove up next to him, wanting to pull him out of the car. He rolled down his window, and I started to scream at him. I sat there full of hate, hoping that he would get out. My wife was begging me to drive away. She became like a distant white noise in the midst of my anger.

Everything about me wanted to get my hands on that man and hurt him. My wife grabbed my arm at one point and tried pinching me to snap me out of it. I didn't feel the pinch because I was so enraged. Curse words came out of me in ways I never wanted my daughter to hear, especially from her father.

The man had enough berating and drove away. I looked at my daughter's face and it was in complete shock; my wife was terrified. Her eyes were full of tears. I looked down and my arm was bleeding because she had been pinching me so hard to get my attention. I had blocked it all out. I had allowed my shadow self to take over.

At once, I was overwhelmed with guilt and shame. That incident had me literally feeling sick for two weeks. Every day, I beat myself up for putting my family at risk like that. What if he had a gun? What if we fought in front of my wife and daughter? *How could I do this? What is the matter with me? Why?!*

**That "why?" indicates a blind spot.** The lack of self-control hints at the existence of a different person living inside of me. This different person is the shadow-self Carl Jung was referring to. Often, we are not aware that we have rejected parts of our personalities. We have suppressed so much about ourselves in order to move past our trauma that these impulsive actions surface at random. During your transition to success, you may find these blind spots and be left with overwhelming guilt and shame because of your actions.

In this chapter, I present a process I discovered to manage my guilt while learning to control my shadow self. Before discovering this process, I utilized self-deprecation in the hopes of correcting my behavior. Constant belittling was destroying my confidence and causing me to make even more mistakes. I didn't realize it at the time, but I was suffering from what has become known as the Dobby Effect.

## THE DOBBY EFFECT

If you are familiar with the Harry Potter series, then you have heard of the domestic elf named Dobby. He is an elf that puts unbelievably high expectations on himself. If Dobby failed, he hurt himself as a form of punishment for not living up to his own expectations. At one point, Dobby can be seen slamming his head into the wall for telling Harry Potter that he had never met a decent wizard.

Like Dobby, I was punishing myself for constantly making mistakes. I wouldn't physically hurt myself; however, emotionally, I was tearing myself to shreds. Especially when that mistake was one that I was working to avoid. Every time I would make that same mistake, I would have fresh guilt compounded with old guilt.

For example, if I got in a road rage incident while heading to work, I wouldn't just feel the guilt from that incident and how I failed to control my temper. I would remember every incident before and feel like a failure. My transition started to feel hopeless. I felt as though there was no getting better. I thought about throwing in the towel.

What would that even look like? I imagined that giving up would be accepting my flaws and no longer working to avoid them. Giving up meant allowing my shadow self to take over. I would just allow my temper and my triggers to run my life. I would embrace them in order to avoid the feeling of guilt and shame. I imagine that there are a lot of people out there who have done just that. I was so close, so many times.

I was finding that no amount of guilt and shame would prevent future outbursts. Guilting myself into submission was not working—in fact, it was making it worse. The more guilt I put on myself, the more fragile my mental health became. I could feel myself getting weaker with every negative outburst. I was putting too much pressure on myself to avoid mistakes and the cracks were showing.

There came a point when I knew, mentally and physically, I couldn't take much more. My mind could not take another mistake because the guilt and shame were becoming too much to bear. That is when I decided on a last-ditch effort to try something new.

# FROM GUILT AND SHAME TO AN ACTION PLAN

During this time, I was journaling about my past (that journal would later become my first book, *Rising Above*). The journaling process was making me realize that my past was not a shameful thing that I should continue to hide, but something to be proud of. This idea that I was somehow better because of my past opened me up to trying something new.

The next outburst came in the form of a verbal altercation with a coworker. I knew I crossed the line, and once again my anger got the best of me. I started to feel the overwhelming sense of guilt that usually accompanied my mistakes. However, this time I was not going to sit and analyze every mistake I made until I felt sick. This time I was going to sit down with a piece of paper and a pen and develop an action plan.

I sat down and wrote about what happened. First, I had to take responsibility, then analyze the event to find ways in which I could have done better. Once I discovered the ways this incident could have been avoided, I decided to plan on using those approaches in the future. So now I had an attack plan for future incidents that would help me to avoid confrontation.

Armed with this plan to do better, I found a mirror. I looked at myself in the mirror and said something that would change my life. I looked myself in the eye and said, "You messed up, but it is okay . . . you are broken—you are doing your best and mistakes will happen. Next time, in order to avoid this mistake, I will do [insert plan of action]." Suddenly, the guilt started to become manageable. The tightening in my chest started to relax enough to breathe, I avoided the panic attack that typically followed one of my outbursts.

I had done everything I could in order to learn from the incident and work toward avoiding it in the future. From that point on, the guilt lost its perceived usefulness. I knew I made a mistake; I took responsibility, I had a plan to avoid it in the future, and then I forgave myself. This was such an unbelievable breakthrough. It was in this moment that I realized I could do this; I could transition into success.

## BREAKING THE CYCLE THROUGH FORGIVENESS

Self-forgiveness is not an easy thing to do. I spent years avoiding it. I opted for self-bullying in the hopes that I could beat myself into submission. I was broken as a child from anger and the absence of love. **I attempted to fight my trauma with the same emotions that broke me.** The reality was that I needed the opposite. I needed to be loved and nurtured. We often think that love is an extrinsic act. I was finding out that it is far more powerful when it comes from within.

When I finally considered self-forgiveness, it shed the mounting pressure to be perfect. This then allowed me to make better decisions, and the positive results seemed to compound.

This is how we use forgiveness to break the cycle.

1. We remember our past and get to know ourselves without rejecting what we do not like. According to Jung's teachings, rejecting parts of ourselves will only create more of a shadow, which leads to blind spots in our actions. These blind spots cause tremendous guilt and shame because they feel out of our control.

2. When we know and embrace ourselves, we retake control of our actions. We can then connect blind spots to repressed trauma and create action plans to avoid the impulsive behavior.
3. We acknowledge that self-forgiveness is a journey and not a single moment or decision.

At this point, you should feel less out of control. You are taking ownership of your past and working to make real changes. **Instead of berating yourself for your mistakes, you are finding root causes so you can work toward self-improvement.** From there, you will cut yourself some slack. You will embrace your brokenness and allow yourself to be human.

## LOVE YOURSELF LIKE YOU'RE SOMEONE YOU LOVE

In order to love someone, you must get to know them. You must spend time with them and listen to them. You pay close attention to what they say and how they are feeling. You ask questions and dig into their past. You find out everything about them so you can understand them on a deeper level. Your goal here is to invest this same energy into yourself. That requires the same hard work you put into loving your spouse, girlfriend, or partner.

When you love someone, you forgive them so much easier. You do so because you know them on a deep level. You know their intentions, despite their potentially contradicting actions. You know their heart and what they meant to do or say, despite their impulsiveness. You see past their mistakes and perceive them for who they really are. Their mistakes are minuscule compared to the goodness you see in them. **You deserve to forgive yourself the same way you forgive the ones you love.**

## TO FORGIVE YOURSELF, KNOW YOURSELF

You can't love someone you don't know; which begs the question: How well do we know ourselves?

I had suppressed so many memories, it was as though my entire childhood didn't exist. I had one or two memories that I allowed to stay. The rest I shoved into a box, and taped, locked, and placed them into a dark corner where I could pretend they weren't real. To this day, phone calls with my brother inevitably lead to us talking about the past, and he reminds me of incidents I had long suppressed. Even after writing a book about my past, I am reminded over and over of more trauma and craziness that existed in our lives.

The only difference is that now that trauma inspires me. It inspires me to help others who are like me. I can use that trauma as a force for good. During the most recent conversation with my brother, he told me a story that made me cry. When you go through your past, you will likely have moments that are hard to cope with. Moments that have been so suppressed that even the memory feels like it happened to someone else. This was a coping mechanism when we were dealing with trauma. That trauma is over—it is time to unpack those boxes and learn to love ourselves. The only way to do that is by getting to know who we are.

You will likely want to hug your younger self. Embrace that feeling; that was you. That feeling is you learning to love yourself. This story makes me want to hug my brother.

During this event I was inside the house and remember the hysteria, but until recently I didn't remember any of the details of the event. I just remember another day with adults fighting and screaming at each other in the front yard . . .

· · · · · · · · · · · · · · · · · · · · · · · · · · ·

My mother had one man in her life my brother and I liked. His name was Paul, and he was the first and last man to treat us like his own sons. I'll never forget him taking us fishing and teaching us how to use a knife. I even remembered asking him if I could call him "Dad." He said yes, and it was the first time I had ever called anyone that in my life. It felt strange, but I loved it.

Paul used to let my brother and me steer his truck on dirt roads. When my brother was driving, I remember putting in a white cassette tape that blared "Ice Ice Baby" by Vanilla Ice. We were having the time of our lives and felt like a real family. It wouldn't take long for something to happen between Paul and my mom, and soon he was gone like the rest of them. Shortly after he left, my mother brought in another man who we hated.

One day while the new guy was at our home, Paul came over to get some of his stuff. We were excited to see him. Unfortunately, my mother's new boyfriend was less than thrilled by his sudden appearance. Paul refused to leave the property until he was given a chance to say bye to my brother and me. My mom's new boyfriend walked outside with a rifle and handed it to my eight-year-old brother and told him to shoot Paul. I can't imagine the fear and confusion running through my brother as he looked at this grown man wanting him to commit murder. My brother became hysterical and told the man he would never do that to Paul. This infuriated my mother's boyfriend who insisted my brother shoot Paul because he was too young to go to jail for murder. My brother was in tears and just kept saying he wouldn't shoot him.

Suddenly, the boyfriend gave up and took aim himself. My brother screamed for Paul to run. Paul jumped in his truck and floored it in reverse. The man shot, hitting the front of Paul's truck.

My brother was asked to kill the first real father figure he had ever had. Then he had to watch him nearly get murdered as he drove away, never to return.

Remembering the event impacted me a great deal. To have someone ask my brother to shoot the one man who treated him like a son breaks my heart. But more importantly, it makes me proud of my brother. He risked his own life at the hands of a psychopath to protect someone he cared about. I am willing to bet that every one of you has had acts of courage in your past. I bet every one of you has a past full of honesty, righteousness, and love. **If you survived poverty, trauma, and abuse, you did so by being brave and powerful.** Remember that along your path of self-forgiveness. Remember all of it.

The broken have this misconception that surviving is merely an act of endurance. That couldn't be further from the truth. Survival is an act of perseverance, resilience, and determination. Imagine the show *Alone*, where contestants are put on an island to survive until the last person is standing. The last thing any of them do is sit there, hoping to survive. They immediately get to work, adapting their mindsets, scanning their surroundings, finding resources, building shelters. They must be incredibly resilient and focused. Surviving trauma and abuse requires the same mental and physical fortitude. **You do not just have a past full of trauma and hardship; you also have a past full of wit, resilience, and courage.**

Forgiving myself for making mistakes was the single most important thing I had ever done. I first had to learn to love and appreciate myself. I did that by digging into my past and giving myself credit for what I overcame. This allowed me to have a better understanding of why I acted out in the first place. Knowing the sources of my anger, anxiety, and automatic negative thoughts helped me to develop an action plan to prevent future outbursts. All of this changed the impact of looking in the mirror and telling myself, "You are broken. You made a mistake. It is okay."

You are going to make mistakes; you are human. Do the work getting to know yourself, so you, too, can look in the mirror and **give that person a break**. Give that person some credit for trying so hard. Lift the thousand pounds off that person's shoulders and allow them to try freely, without the fear of failure. Nobody can forgive you but you.

# Chapter 7

# THE VICTIM

"[The drifter] will lack enthusiasm and initiative to begin anything he is not forced to undertake, and he will plainly express his weakness by taking the line of least resistance whenever he can do so."
—Napoleon Hill

Living in poverty attempts to create victims out of all of us. It may feel easier to live believing that life is something that is completely out of your control. However, the lack of progress will always rest on your shoulders. The victim mentality is a way for those who have given up to numb the pain of their decisions.

The number one thing standing between you and your transition to success is your mindset. *Better Broken* is the title of this book for a reason—it is a mindset that allows us to focus on the positive aspects of our trauma. It is an empowering statement that should give survivors hope that they can use their trauma for greatness. The worst thing we can do is allow ourselves to become perpetual victims or develop what some psychologists refer to as "the tendency for interpersonal victimhood" (TIV).

In this chapter, we will break down TIV and learn to identify victimhood mindsets. Your growth will not only depend on not developing a victimhood mindset, but it will also require you to identify it in others. Victimhood mindsets are contagious and eat away at our ability to create a positive perception of reality. If we fail to recognize these patterns of behavior in others, we can be pulled down by their negativity.

## THE TENDENCY FOR INTERPERSONAL VICTIMHOOD

The tendency for interpersonal victimhood is defined by Rahav Gabay and her colleagues as "*an ongoing feeling that the self is a victim, which is generalized across many kinds of relationships. As a result, victimization becomes a central part of the individual's identity.*"[13] (Italics added.)

This is where things become grim for those who have a perpetual victimhood mindset. According to the research, they tend to have an "external locus of control." In other words, they believe that **they have little to no control over their lives, but are instead a product of fate, luck, and the actions of others**.

Everything about self-improvement revolves around focusing on what *is* in our control. If we believe that nothing is in our control, then we just allow life to dictate our paths. This lackadaisical floating can become what Napoleon Hill refers to as *drifting*. In one of my favorite books, *Outwitting the Devil*, Hill refers to drifting as the most common cause of failure in any walk of life.

Hill's description of a "drifter" includes a lack of self-confidence, little or no imagination, no enthusiasm or initiative. According to Hill, a drifter has "a total lack of a major purpose in life . . . He will never accomplish anything requiring thought and effort." "A drifter also spends more than he makes, and follows the path of least resistance whenever possible." A drifter will also have a personality "without magnetism" and opinions on everything but "accurate knowledge of nothing." Finally, "He may be jack of all trades but good at none. He will neglect to cooperate with those around him, even those on whom he must depend for food and shelter," Hill continues, and it doesn't get more flattering for the drifter.

If you can identify some of yourself in this definition, it is time to start taking responsibility and creating momentum in your life.

- - - - - - - - - - - - - - - - - - - - -

It is my belief that Hill's drifter is synonymous with someone who has embraced a victimhood mindset. Someone who believes that they have no control over their circumstances *will* become victim to them. Just as a driver *will* become a victim of a car accident if he lets go of the wheel.

Before we move on to avoiding the victimhood mindset, let's continue to evaluate the recent clinical observations and research conducted by Rahav Gabay and her team. The more we understand about the tendency for interpersonal victimhood, the better we will be at identifying and avoiding it.

According to the research, both individual and collective victimhood are composed of four dimensions:

1. Need for recognition
2. Moral elitism
3. Lack of empathy
4. Rumination

If you have a strong association with any of these dimensions or experience victimhood in interpersonal encounters, you would be considered a high-TIV individual, which means "likely to be associated with individuals' sensitivity to both actual and potential hurtful behaviors, and expectations of hurtful behavior in ambiguous circumstances."[14]

Every situation involving interpersonal relations is ambiguous. So much of our contact with other people is open to whatever interpretation we choose. It is important to understand that if you are a high-TIV individual, you will naturally heighten the significance of negative encounters.

## BEING A HIGH-TIV INDIVIDUAL

I am a high-TIV individual and constantly assume the worst when it comes to interpersonal contacts. I frequently find myself seeking counsel before acting on these assumptions. I understand this about myself, so I avoid making quick judgment calls about others based solely on my interpretations of the encounter. Instead, I contact my inner circle to confirm my beliefs. My inner circle generally disagrees with me and feels that the situation is far less sinister than I imagined. Acknowledging my shortcomings has allowed me to find solutions instead of destroying relationships over misconceptions.

I have no doubt that if I hadn't chosen growth to cope with my trauma, I would have become a perpetual victim and spent my life drifting and blaming others. Let's analyze the four dimensions and see if we can identify ourselves or others in them. It is important to identify drifting not only in ourselves but others as well. This will allow us to practice avoidance and safeguard our growth.

**The first is the need for recognition.** Victims with a need for recognition strongly desire to have their victimhood acknowledged and empathized with by others. The idea is that the victim's perception of the world has been off-balanced by a trauma. They feel recognition of that trauma will reestablish their previous beliefs of justice and fairness. The perpetual victim will likely continue to seek retribution from perceived perpetrators and compassion from others—in other words, a rebalancing is very unlikely.

I have personally experienced living with this type of victim as a child. This victim becomes obsessed with finding perpetrators and constantly seeks justice and empathy. Their life becomes about finding the worst in people and wanting them to feel guilt over their "wrongdoings." You will know when you meet someone like this because they always have a villain to destroy. Whether it is an ex-spouse, family member, neighbor, or stranger, there is always someone who did something morally egregious that needs to pay. If you are not the villain, they will seek your empathy and try to recruit you to their cause. If drugs and alcohol enter the picture, their desire for retribution can become emotionally and physically violent.

**Next is moral elitism—this victimhood mentality gives the victim "the perception of immaculate morality."** According to psychologist Scott Kaufman, "Moral elitism often develops as a defense mechanism against deeply painful emotions as a way to maintain a positive self-image."[15] Like Carl Jung's theory of the shadow self or Freud's theory of projection, the moral elitist may be rejecting their destructive impulses and projecting them onto others.

The moral elitist wants desperately to view themselves as a good person. In order to do so, they categorize everyone else as either good or evil. They then manipulate the metrics for good depending on their own actions . . . essentially playing a game while changing the rules in order to win.

It is my assumption that their projection stems from a frequency bias that causes them to face their actions in others. This is known as the Baader-Meinhof phenomenon. The perfect example of this is when you buy a new car and suddenly you start to see the same model all over the place. The abundance of that model hasn't suddenly increased; only your awareness of it has.

The moral elitists' awareness of their negative behavior has increased. Now they see that behavior more often in others. This angers them because they are trying to live under the false pretense that their actions are justified. This leads to defensive projection or getting mad at others to avoid taking responsibility.

**The third victimhood dimension is lack of empathy, or "a preoccupation with one's own suffering and a decreased attention and concern about others."** This lack of empathy prevents the victim from acknowledging that there are others who have had it worse. This causes them to exaggerate their own suffering to the point of denial. This doesn't allow them to have an accurate perception of suffering. They believe their life is worse, their situation is worse, and they were treated more poorly than anyone.

When I was growing up, empathy helped me get through hard times. I acknowledged that there were people out there who had it far worse than me. I had met many of them. I met siblings whose parents left them to live in an abandoned shack with no electricity or food. Two of the boys I grew up with are currently serving life sentences for murder.

Convincing yourself that your situation is worse than anyone else's prevents you from seeing how truly good you have it. Allowing yourself to see the atrocities in this world can be a source of great appreciation for your circumstances.

**The last dimension is rumination, which is defined as "a focus of attention on the symptoms of one's distress, and its possible causes and consequences rather than its possible solutions."** To ruminate means to think deeply on something.

Do you choose to think deeply on becoming the person you wish to be? Or do you think deeply on negative thoughts outside of your control?

I have allowed myself to dwell on situations from the past so much that I have become sick with guilt. When I was in Special Forces, I attached an M320 grenade launcher to my side. I didn't have a mount for it, so I made one myself. The mount ran through the trigger guard of the grenade launcher.

It is never a good idea to run anything through the trigger guard due to the possibility of an accidental discharge. However, I was sure I would leave it unloaded until I was ready to fire it. The weapon was meant as a backup to my primary rifle. I carried a bandolier of explosive rounds around my waist.

Within minutes of our first combat operation in Afghanistan, we started to take contact. I loaded the grenade launcher to shoot. Just then another operator yelled that he had a better position. I reattached the grenade launcher to my side—it was now loaded with a high-explosive round with the safety on. When I arrived at the operator's position, it was on top of a roof with no ladder. The operator pulled me up by my right arm, which caused my side to scrape up the wall. This pushed the safety selector down to fire, and simultaneously pulled the cord attaching the launcher to my side. The launcher went off and the grenade punched a hole through the floor. If it weren't for the minimum arming distance, the round would have exploded, possibly killing myself and the guy below me.

Despite neither of those realities coming to fruition, I could not stop dwelling on the potential negative outcome I had almost caused. It took the better part of a year before I stopped dreaming about a family crying at the loss of their father and husband at my hands. It took about two years before I chose to stop dwelling on the event. I was putting myself through hell for something I could not change. I was ruminating on the possible consequences of my mistakes instead of finding solutions. I couldn't change the past; however, one solution is using the event to teach others and help them avoid similar mistakes.

The broken have suffered a great deal of pain. It should come as no surprise that we want to avoid as much of that pain as possible in the future. However, we must always take responsibility for how we choose to avoid that pain and cope with our issues. Remember that the "T" in TIV stands for "tendency." Having tendencies does not make you a perpetual victim. It is when you continually hide behind those tendencies and refuse to acknowledge them that they become who you are.

## THE THREE LITTLE PIGS

I've always appreciated Jordan Peterson's ability to relate real-world circumstances to fairy tales. There is something powerful about looking at a story we all know and seeing it from a different perspective. It is the essence of avoiding victimhood mentalities, taking the same information and choosing an alternate perspective.

Let's look at the fairy tale of "The Three Little Pigs." In the story, the mother pig sends her three children off into the world to fend for themselves. The three pigs all have enough sense to prioritize building shelters given the delicacy of bacon and the presence of wolves.

Two of the pigs build flimsy shelters out of straw and sticks, respectively. These weak constructs offer a false sense of security from the wolf. But, instead of facing their fears and thinking about the wolf, they choose to distract themselves by dancing and playing. Distraction prevents deep thought; deep thought would have forced them to confront the dangers of their environment.

I believe the wolf represents life. Life brings with it unescapable hardship, but it also brings opportunity; we all get to choose what we focus on.

The first two pigs choose to focus on hardship: wolves have large fangs, they love pork, and apparently they have strong lungs. The two pigs respond to their fear through avoidance. They choose to build shelters that merely give the appearance of safety. Their unwillingness to face the wolf prevents them from knowing its weaknesses. They allow themselves to become victims by ignoring their reality.

The third pig chooses to acknowledge the wolf. This allows him to think deeply about the wolf's existence. Facing his fears gives him the ability to understand the wolf on a deeper level. He can evaluate his behavior patterns and weaknesses. He then creates a house that can withstand the wolf so he doesn't have to live in fear.

Finally, the wolf comes knocking. The first two pigs are forced to face their decisions. Their weak shelters fall with ease, they become victims, and they blame the wolf. This may have made them feel better, but the result was the same: running away, begging to be saved by others.

The wolf arrives at the home of the third pig, who concocts an ingenious plan to capture him. He entices the wolf into coming down the chimney and has a pot of boiling water waiting for him.

Because the third pig prepared mentally and emotionally for this event, his cognitive abilities remain intact.

The third pig is anything but a victim. He captures the wolf, cooks him, and eats him for supper. The third pig is able to identify that hardship is always accompanied by opportunity. **He chooses to look at the meat of the wolf rather than the fangs.**

That is the situation that we are all in. It is the same wolf. So how do we see the wolf as dinner, while others only see a predator? How do we become the person who stands their ground instead of running for help?

**The answer is choosing growth over victimhood.** This allows us to prepare for life and stand firm when hard times come. The first two pigs worked only to give the appearance of success. Everyone will face tragedy and defeat in life, and when they do, appearances will be useless. How we come out of those situations will entirely depend on the mentalities we choose going into them. We can choose to play mental tricks on ourselves in order to avoid responsibility, or we can choose to work hard and become the best version of ourselves possible. The key is understanding that there is a choice, and every choice has a consequence.

Consider what cognitive psychologist Scott Barry Kaufman has to say: "If socialization processes can instill in individuals a victimhood mindset, then surely the very same processes can instill in people a personal growth mindset."[16]

Kaufman also asks what would happen if we all learned as children that our traumas don't have to define us and that trauma and victimhood can be experienced, yet not form the core of who we are.

## POST-TRAUMATIC GROWTH

I believe that broken people have obtained a harnessable power through their suffering. When this power is harnessed, others will say they have the "it" factor, or charisma, as German sociologist Max Weber defines it: "A certain quality of an individual personality, by virtue of which he is set apart from ordinary men and treated as endowed with supernatural, superhuman, or at least specifically exceptional powers or qualities."[17]

This supernatural gift is often viewed as a happenstance. Some people are blessed with it while others are not. **It is my belief that this supernatural gift is developed through hardship.** Once undesirable traits are harnessed and refined, the broken can start tapping into this gift.

The negative effects of trauma have been meticulously studied for many years; however, the term "post-traumatic growth" is comparatively new. Before researchers studied the benefits of trauma, they primarily focused on the negative effects, such as personality, anxiety, and depressive disorders.

I can imagine how many people failed to reach their potential because of this. They were led to believe that all that derived from their trauma was psychological damage. **It is time that we emphasize the positive.**

The sooner the broken embrace the positive, the sooner they can change their perspective and correct negative neural pathways. Neural pathways are superhighways of nerve cells transmitting data. The more electrical data sent on a particular highway, the more solidified into our existence it becomes. Thankfully, neuroplasticity will allow us to redirect those highways. This will allow us to start focusing on growth and having a more positive outlook on our situations.

So, what is post-traumatic growth?

According to professor of psychology Richard Glenn Tedeschi and his colleague Lawrence Calhoun, it is "the experience of positive change that occurs as a result of the struggle with highly challenging life crisis." They go on to say that it manifests in several ways, including "an increased appreciation for life in general, more meaningful interpersonal relationships, an increased sense of personal strength, changed priorities, and a richer existential and spiritual life."[18]

How do we obtain post-traumatic growth? It is a process, and all the steps in this book are geared toward that process. Reducing negativity and stress, creating safe environments, identifying and prioritizing triggers . . . All of these things are incrementally moving us toward post-traumatic growth and away from victimhood mentalities. Each step is redirecting negative pathways into positive ones.

## POSITIVITY MINING

One of the techniques that helped me achieve this is something I call "positivity mining." Actual mining is the process of extracting useful material from the earth. It is laborious and difficult work. Miners have to wade through tons of useless dirt and rock to find the precious material they are looking for.

I like to think of mining because always seeking positivity is hard work. Reminding myself of this allows me to stick with it when I want to focus on negativity. Like a miner, you must work past the useless material and know where the veins of gold run. You must be patient and continue to chip away knowing that there is precious material within it.

Every situation you encounter in life is the same. It is mostly useless junk that needs to be avoided, but deep within that junk lies precious material, jewels in the form of understanding and perspective. If you are willing to do the work, you can mine positivity from every situation you encounter.

Recently, I was in the running to host a Netflix show about Special Operations. We had gone through about six months of phone calls, Skype meetings, and even an in-person personality screen test. For the screen test, the final five got together for a weekend of events that would be recorded and sent back to the production company and then on to Netflix. From that footage, they would choose their host.

I finally got the call and was told I got passed on by Netflix. I was hurt. I had always wanted to host an actual show, and I was so close to getting it I could taste it. I allowed myself to be upset for a couple minutes, and then I got to work positivity mining the situation.

My company had just started to pick up steam, and this show would require me to travel. I knew that by taking this spot I would be putting my company's growth at risk. So, I decided instead to turn this rejection into an opportunity.

I thought about how long it would take from the start of filming to air. I guessed about a year before I was watching the show on television. That gave me one year to push my business so hard that by the time that show aired it would have been an obvious step backwards. Suddenly, I felt like I was back in control. I had just taken all the power away from Netflix and put it back into my hands.

This is the same mental approach I took after walking in on my first wife in bed with another man. I thought about the man she had cheated on, then I thought about the man I could become. I wanted to turn the worst situation of my life into an opportunity. I would look back on that day and know that she started me down a path of growth instead of self-destruction.

So, I got to work getting my act together. I wasn't going to pick up the pieces and move on. I was going to develop so much post-traumatic growth that her cheating on me would be the best thing that ever happened to me. As it turned out, it was just the spark I needed.

Both scenarios required me to positivity mine the situation and then create the most beneficial outcome. Sometimes the obvious choice requires you to put in work. You must use some creative thinking to turn the situation into an opportunity, and then be willing to follow through with your plan. You can use the traumatic experience to motivate your growth. That way, when you look back on hard times, you appreciate them because they were a catalyst for improvement.

## Chapter 8

# FINANCIAL PITFALLS

> "Live like no one else now, so later you can
> live and give like no one else."
> **—Dave Ramsey**

Now that we have focused on our behavioral growth, it's time to talk money. It goes without saying that every one of us who chooses to transition from poverty to success will want to avoid being broke again. It is hard to focus on achieving your goals with no financial literacy. It's difficult to stop allowing money to control your actions and to, instead, learn to use it like the tool it is. This chapter focuses on the financial pitfalls that nearly derailed my transition and ways to avoid your own pitfalls.

So, why do the poor stay poor? Some research suggests there is a poverty line that limits opportunity for advancement for those born beneath it, while other researchers feel that people living in poverty lack the advanced skills required to do higher-paying jobs.

Having been born into poverty, I suspect the issue lies in a multitude of reasons. Those range from low self-expectations to a lack of fundamental knowledge of money management. When you grow up poor, you focus on obtaining money to solve your problems. The best way to combat poverty is by obtaining more money. Unfortunately, even those who obtain more money will often lose it due to financial illiteracy.

Throughout our lives in poverty, we were taught lessons that created a poverty mentality. This poverty mindset developed from not believing that our futures were worth investing in. From living every day as though tomorrow will not be better, and the fear that more may never come, we learn to use money as a form of escapism. According to the Oxford English Dictionary, escapism is defined as "the tendency to seek distraction and relief from unpleasant realities, especially by seeking entertainment or engaging in fantasy."

## THE MONEY FANTASY

What is the fantasy of those living in poverty? To have money and buy things that wealthy people buy. So, despite their financial situation, any influx of money is immediately spent on living that fantasy. These fantasies are usually in the form of money traps like new cars, clothes, and whatever else will make us feel better about our situations. Typically, things that are expensive immediately give off the appearance of financial freedom.

These items become traps that hold people back from working toward their desired future. They hold them back with looming debt and eat away at their income until they have nothing left to invest in themselves. If you have nothing in savings, your ability to take risks is limited. If things are eating away at your ability to save, how will you buy time to work toward your dreams? Investing in yourself nearly always requires time, and time costs money.

When I mention buying time, I mean covering expenses while you work toward your dreams. Whether you are starting your own company or changing career paths, you will likely need money to float your bills during transitions.

These pitfalls keep people from achieving more in life by preventing them from having enough reserves to buy themselves some time.

It is difficult to live in poverty and not focus on social status. I used to dream of driving nice cars and being treated with respect instead of being looked at like trash. I thought having nice things would elevate my status and treatment.

Maybe a new car would give me a feeling of achievement. I watched people buying new cars and was jealous of their advancement in life. That is, until I saw that car become one of their biggest stressors. Their payments were always too high and left them with little money for anything else. The minute anything happened that required money, they couldn't afford to make their payments. There is nothing worse than praying you get one more day before the repo man comes to collect your only transportation.

## MY DEBT

Credit card debt is another major trap that prevents people from achieving more in life. Credit cards offer an immediate escape through purchasing whatever our hearts desire. You want to look like you have money? Get a credit card. Get what you want and worry about the payments later. Not only is this practice common, but it is also encouraged to "build your credit history." Like many others, I was under the impression that I had to get credit cards and use them to start building my credit score. Despite having avoided the new vehicle trap, the credit cards got me.

The funny thing was, I never even knew why I needed a credit score. I didn't know anything about scores, interest rates, or even how to check my full report. It wasn't until I became completely overwhelmed in debt that I finally started to research. By the time I started studying credit scores and how they were tracked, and got a grasp on interest rates, it was too late. My credit score was destroyed. I was thousands of dollars in debt and more than ninety days past due on all my accounts.

The debt collectors were starting to wear me down. I found myself dealing with extreme anxiety any time my phone rang. I realized that I preferred looking broke than dealing with creditors and the stress of being in debt. After joining the Army, I started getting my first real paychecks. Of course, I wanted to blow the money immediately, but fortunately, I had no time because I had to finish Airborne School and then go to Ranger Assessment and Selection Program (RASP).

This delay allowed me to accumulate $5,000 in my bank account. I remember standing in front of the Ranger barracks checking my account on my phone. I had never seen that much money before. Just as I started to get excited about all the things I could buy, my phone rang. It was a creditor who bought my debt from the bank and wanted the $10,000 I owed him.

At that moment, I made a financial decision that would begin to change the way I looked at money. I decided that I would rather go without than deal with this stress again. I told the debt collector I had $5,000 to my name, take it or leave it. He laughed and said I owed him twice that much. I hung up the phone and went back to the barracks. Two days later, the same debt collector called back. All he said was, "I'll take the $5,000."

And just like that . . . I was debt free! Of course, having all my debt go to collections destroyed my credit. But at least now I could start making better financial decisions and avoid getting in that situation again. From that point, I changed the way I viewed money and started to learn as much as I could. I listened to books like *Rich Dad Poor Dad* and Dave Ramsey's *Total Money Makeover*. Becoming financially literate gave me the ability to chase my dreams.

## CHANGE THE POVERTY MINDSET

If you want to use your brokenness for the life of your dreams, it will require you to be financially stable. You will have to develop a base knowledge of money to get out of poverty and never look back. People who are born into poverty often stay there because they fail to learn how to make money work for them.

If we are going to break the cycle of poverty, it is time to change our mindset about money and how to use it. **Money is a tool that should be used to achieve future goals.** It should never be used as a form of escapism because we are unhappy. If we are unhappy with our current situation, we need to plan a better one—a future we can be excited about, one that allows us to live up to our potential. Then we can choose to embrace that future instead of buying momentary happiness.

In order to embrace *your* future, you need to believe in it. You need to have faith that you can make that dream a reality. The best plan in the world will fail if you don't believe in it enough to try. You will have to reject the actions of those around you and start living differently. Poverty makes us feel as though survival is the only option. That is only true if we embrace that mentality instead of believing that we deserve more and are willing to work for it.

If we live in poverty and no longer desire to, why would we mimic the actions of others living in poverty? Would that not just create the same habits that keep *them* there? We need to live like no one else so later we can live like no one else.

So how do we change our poverty mindset to one of success and growth? **We reprioritize the things that we value. We stop giving value to things easily earned and start valuing things that are hard to obtain.** It will never be hard to walk into a dealership and sign papers. It is never difficult to swipe a credit card and be handed a new shiny thing. Those things will never give you value because anyone can do them. **The things that will give you value are inherently difficult.**

For example, being fit, having an education (formal or informal), being skilled at a craft, financial freedom . . . these are all things that should be valued over new cars, new shoes, and the latest trends. **The goal of financial intelligence is to move freely throughout life without feeling stuck. It is not to acquire more money to buy more things.**

. . . . . . . . . . . . . . . . . . . . . . . . . .

The day I hit the streets as a police officer, I knew the job wasn't for me. I tried to find greater fulfillment through promotion and hard work. I got on an impact team but still felt unfulfilled professionally. The 2020 Denver riots were an eye-opener for a lot of police officers, most of whom talked about moving on from police work and chasing their dreams.

I was one of the dreamers who wanted to be my own boss and start my own business. I listened to dozens of officers talk about their dream careers and how they would love to go after them. Nearly all of those officers are still cops today. Years of poor financial decisions limited their freedom. They had spent so many years buying momentary happiness that they accumulated too much debt. They couldn't afford to buy time to transition into their dream careers.

When everyone else was driving new cars to work, I drove an old Subaru Forester that shot white smoke out of the exhaust and leaked oil. I had to put a quart of oil a week in that thing to keep the engine from blowing. Once, in the middle of summer, I was stuck in traffic, and the car decided to stall in the fast lane. I sat there stuck on the side of the road looking as broke as ever. I was making great money, but there I was stranded on the side of the road. After about twenty attempts, the car fired back up and got me to work.

When I got to work, my coworkers laughed. They couldn't imagine why I would drive that car while earning nearly six figures. I saw the picture much differently. I saw every dollar as a minute I could buy back in the future. The more I saved, the longer I could go without a job while I built my business. **When I changed the way I viewed money, I started to see their shiny new toys as weights holding them down.** My crappy car became a sense of pride, a constant reminder of sacrificing now for later.

I wasn't the only officer who treated money this way. One day, I met an older day-shift sergeant. Something was different about him.

For one thing, unlike the other sergeants, he seemed happy. That was a strange thing for an old crusty sergeant on the verge of retirement. Usually, they are all full of hate and anger and counting the days till they depart. Yet this guy just sat there in his old Walmart dad shoes and his sun-worn uniform like the world was his oyster.

I later found out that he also prided himself on his frugalness. He chose to invest his money in real estate instead of fancy cars and boats. This unassuming sergeant was sitting there without a care in the world. His salary was well over six figures, and he was a multimillionaire from real estate investing. The carefree vibe he put off was the self-confidence of a man free to walk out that door the minute anyone crossed him.

It is a powerful thing to be free. Too many of us are tied to our jobs regardless of how much we hate them or how bad they treat us. Yet when we choose to change our perspective on money, we can live in a way that gives us that freedom. Freedom to walk out of a job you hate and toward one that you love.

When I decided to get out of the military and join the police force, I was going to take a $30,000-a-year pay cut. The only reason I was able to take this pay cut was because I stayed debt free and saved enough money to cover bills until I was promoted. I was saving to buy time so I could do what I wanted to do.

## CHANGING THE WAY YOU LOOK AT MONEY

It took me years to understand that my socioeconomic status could not be changed with money. Sure, money is a single metric that can be utilized to determine a person's status in life. However, I believe it is the *wrong* metric. **People are far more complex than their bank accounts.** The true metrics for societal status should be hard work, dedication, commitment, self-awareness, and wisdom. These are all things that must be obtained and cannot be passed on or gifted. Money is a tool that everyone should know how to use; it is not a judge of character, morals, or success.

Having this understanding will change the way you look at money, ultimately changing the way you spend it. Money is a powerful tool that can make you a powerful person. However, having it is not where the power is derived... controlling it is. Everyone has access to money, and how they control a little will determine how they control a lot.

You don't need to become a financial expert to thrive in this world. You just need to know the major pitfalls that could derail your path to success. If you want to avoid all of them, understand that debt is your enemy. The closer you can live to being debt free, the less stress and anxiety you will have and the more freedom you will have to change your career path and take risks.

The major pitfalls will always be attached to purchasing things you cannot afford. To avoid this, it is important to understand why you want those things in the first place. This is where the mindset shift will come into effect and make avoiding debt easier. **Get to the root cause of why you feel a new car or new things will make you better. There are numerous ways that broken people cope with trauma.**

Buying things to make ourselves feel better can be one of them. Emotional spending, or retail therapy, can set you down a path that you never recover from.

So, dig deep into your past and find the moments that make you feel insecure about who you are. What void are you trying to fill? I never wanted to feel poor again, and I thought nice things would give me more value. The only things that ever gave me more value were things I worked hard to earn. I can't stress this enough: **you cannot purchase self-appreciation.**

You can earn self-appreciation by doing difficult things that make you proud of what you have achieved. Saving money is difficult, avoiding emotional spending is difficult, and avoiding lifestyle creep is difficult, but these things will bring you a sense of pride and accomplishment. Purchasing things will only be a momentary high followed by guilt and shame. The debt will loom over your head like a dark cloud. The more debt, the lower the cloud, until it feels like it is sitting on your head making it hard to breathe.

Adding money to poor financial habits will only delay the inevitable. One study suggests that lottery winners are more likely to declare bankruptcy within three to five years than the average American. With a third of winners declaring bankruptcy after their windfall, it becomes clear that simply adding money is not the solution.[21]

Lottery winners are not the only examples of this. Celebrities who have made millions over the course of their careers have had to file for bankruptcy. Some of these celebrities include 50 Cent, Wesley Snipes, Nicolas Cage, and Burt Reynolds. Chris Tucker was, at one point, the highest-paid actor in Hollywood. He earned over 48 million dollars for the Rush Hour franchise alone. Fast-forward to 2021, and the actor is facing a lawsuit for reportedly owing the IRS over nine million dollars in unpaid taxes.

In his autobiography, *I Can't Make This Up,* Kevin Hart is open about his money struggles, which landed him broke and owing the IRS hundreds of thousands of dollars in back taxes. Kevin was spending everything he was making on things with quickly depreciating values and trying to give the appearance of success. He didn't understand how to manage his money, so when he got it, it nearly ruined him. That is what we want to avoid. **Learn enough about money so that it doesn't ruin you when it comes.**

- - -

You are in the process of applying the lessons you learned from trauma, neglect, and poverty to societal success. Because of your background, there is a far greater chance that you will achieve that success. The broken chase their passions because it provides purpose and meaning—two things that greatly counter the negative effects of trauma and abuse. What the broken don't always realize is that money will often be a by-product of that pursuit.

Your eagerness and drive will get you to your goals. The question is, *Will you be ready?* When the money comes, will you use it as a tool to create more freedom? Or will the money ruin you and create the same caged feeling as poverty?

The choice is yours. You must choose to believe in yourself. Only then will you start acting like your success is coming and start preparing. The best preparation is knowledge. Kevin Hart's lack of knowledge nearly ruined him. He was not about to make that mistake again, and he became one of the most financially literate celebrities on the planet. Knowledge is key. It is vital that you obtain that knowledge *now* and not wait till the money comes, or it may be too late.

You need to:

- Study credit scores and how they work.
- Learn how to get debt free and stay that way.

- Learn how to manage a small amount of money so you can manage a large amount when it comes.
- Read books like *Total Money Makeover*, *Rich Dad Poor Dad*, and *Think and Grow Rich*.
- Utilize your bank's online credit report tools that allow you to track positive and negative strikes against your account.
- Start analyzing the financial mentalities of those around you. Learn to identify what decisions are holding them back. What choices are making their future lives harder for momentary relief? The sooner you can identify these roadblocks, the sooner you can avoid them.

When you start to get the hang of money, it gets a lot easier to save more and spend less. Every penny saved is an opportunity to buy a minute of time. That time could be spent chasing your passions, changing careers, or just not stressing over debt. We have suffered enough at the hands of others; we broken don't need to be the cause of our own downfalls. Most of our suffering is avoidable with a little knowledge and hard work. Let's put an end to the poverty mindset and live like no one else, so later we can live like no one else.

# Chapter 9

# POWER OF READING

"People do not decide their futures, they decide their habits and their habits decide their futures."
—F. M. Alexander

Now that you have gotten your behavioral and financial goals in place, it is time to get educated. One thing that is always left by the wayside in poverty is education. Education is extremely low on the totem pole when our lives are spent in a state of survival. The transition from poverty to success requires us to educate ourselves and become experts in our desired fields. The best way to do that is through reading books. Books hold the key to everything we want to achieve in life.

In fact, there seems to be a connection between highly successful people and a love for reading—from former presidents to athletes and celebrities. Amazon started as an online bookstore, which allowed Jeff Bezos to pursue his passion for reading and become one of the world's wealthiest individuals.

No matter where you look, it seems that those who reach the highest levels of society love to read. Is this a coincidence? Or is reading the key to unlocking untapped potential? In this chapter, we will analyze some research to determine how books are unlocking greatness, and how you can start taking advantage of this resource used by the most influential people in history.

## **THE ART OF TRANSPORTATION**

Growing up, books were never a part of my life. I preferred to spend my time running around the desert causing trouble. Whether it was smashing windows of abandoned houses or throwing dirt clods at passing cars, I always wanted to replicate the chaos in my life through my actions. According to professors at the University of Toronto, "a child's behavior is an outward manifestation of inner stability and security."[22]

I had no inner stability or security; my life was a powder keg that would randomly go off every two to three days. Then one day, in middle school, I got into yet another fight and was placed on suspension for three days. My aunt thought it would be a good idea to take me to my grandparents' house in Ontario. She knew that I enjoyed being suspended because I could do what I wanted instead of going to school. So she took me somewhere where that wasn't possible.

I got to my grandparents' and turned on the TV, ready to enjoy my three-day vacation. My aunt walked in, shut the television off, and handed me a book called *Harry Potter and the Sorcerer's Stone*. She told me that I would spend the entire day reading or sitting quietly, but TV was out. I protested by sitting in that spot in silence for what seemed like hours. Finally, my ADHD became too much to bear and I cracked open the book.

Suddenly, I found myself completely lost in the story. My imagination was firing on all cylinders. I had unknowingly spent hours pleasure reading for the first time in my life. Before that day, the only time I read was in a special reading class at school for kids who were struggling to keep up.

That class was the first time that I realized I could barely read. I remember the teacher telling me a number that coincided with a section of books in the library. The numbers separated the books into grade levels. Every time she gave me a number from which to choose my books, it was several years behind my grade.

When I protested reading children's books, she handed me one from my grade and asked me to read a chapter out loud. She stood there staring at me as I struggled to pronounce the words. I had to fight back tears as I handed the book back, accepting that I couldn't read it.

Yet when I started to read Harry Potter, not knowing a lot of the words didn't matter. I could simply skip words because the world was forming in my imagination. It was alive and happening in real time. My imagination didn't need every word. It just needed enough to weave the story together. For the first time, I saw the power of reading. Harry Potter allowed me to transition out of my pain and suffering and into a story that captured my imagination in every way.

During that suspension, I read the first two Harry Potter books. I had gone from zero finished books to two in three days. I had gone from zero pleasure reading to over sixteen hours. Most importantly, I learned the art of transportation or the act of losing yourself in a book, which research suggests is very good for you. According to Melanie Green, PhD, professor at the University of Buffalo, one of the benefits of reading is that "stories allow us to feel connected with others and part of something bigger than ourselves."[23]

This coincides with the work done by Keith Oatley, PhD, professor in the department of applied psychology and human development at the University of Toronto, which found that reading fiction allows us to connect with characters and stories so different from our own that we can increase levels of empathy and understanding, which can then be applied to real-world scenarios.[24] Oatley states, "In these narrative worlds, we experience a simulated reality and feel real emotions in response to the conflicts and relationships of story characters." This "simulation" holds real consequences for our social world and may help improve social skills, including empathy.

The idea that books may improve empathy and social understanding is a profound discovery. The ability to feel what others feel is a key to success in life. To be a great leader you must empathize in order to inspire and take care of people. To be a great spouse requires you to feel what your partner feels, so you can support and care for them. To be a great tactician in war, you must empathize with your enemy so you can understand their motivations and decisions.

## CONNECTING TO YOUR FUTURE SELF

Once I learned how powerful my imagination could be, I started to experiment with it. I imagined my desired future in such detail that I could transport to it and feel happiness. Books taught me to use my imagination with such vibrance that my imagined future felt real. This realness caused me to make decisions in the present that would influence my trajectory toward that future.

This connectedness to my future self created a sense of responsibility for future me. My future self became someone I wanted to look out for. Consider what eighteenth-century philosopher Joseph Butler said on the topic:

*For if the self or person of today, and that of tomorrow, are not the same, but only like persons, the person of today is really no more interested in what will befall the person of tomorrow, than in what will befall any other person.*

Butler's research has since been expanded upon by Hal Hershfield, professor at the University of California. Hershfield's studies have shown that those who have a deeper connection to their future selves tend to have more money in savings and better physical health. According to Hershfield, "If people are better connected to their future selves, then they're going to have an enhanced ability to recognize the consequences of their present-day decisions on their future selves."[25]

Imagining your future self with enough detail to create someone you care about is difficult. It requires constant utilization of your imagination, and you can expand the power of your imagination through reading.

## My Reading List

Finding the right authors is crucial. For me, it was Aldous Huxley and his *Brave New World*, written in 1932, or George Orwell and his *1984* and *Animal Farm*.

If dystopian science fiction is not your thing, try Ernest Hemingway's *A Farewell to Arms*, or one of my favorite authors of all time, Anthony Bourdain and his *Kitchen Confidential* and *The Nasty Bits*. If you like Bourdain's style you may also enjoy the work of Hunter S. Thompson. I really enjoyed *Fear and Loathing in Las Vegas* and his work on the Hells Angels titled *Hell's Angels: The Strange and Terrible Saga of the Outlaw Motorcycle Gangs*.

Another favorite is Paulo Coelho's *The Alchemist*, a fictional tale of a young man's journey to find his treasure. This book is beautifully written, and the message is so powerful it moved me to follow my heart and pursue my treasure no matter what. *The Alchemist* is perfectly paired with James Allen's *As a Man Thinketh*, which illustrates how to change your circumstances by first changing the way you think.

The key here is understanding that everyone is different and every author speaks to people differently. It can take time to find authors that stretch your imagination and enhance your ability to think through their writing styles and topics. Once you do, it will become clear that there is no better medium for wisdom, thought, and imagination.

> However, remember that an author's true intention is to make you feel. Whether that feeling is inspiration or entertainment, the work should have a genuine impact on you. If instead it feels like a chore, put it down and find a new one. My bookshelf has dozens of *New York Times* bestsellers that I will never finish. I don't care how many copies it sold; if it's not moving or entertaining me, I move on.

## NONFICTION IN THE MORNING, FICTION AT NIGHT

There is a technique to utilizing fiction and nonfiction cohesively that I learned from reading Tim Ferriss. The technique is to read nonfiction in the morning and fiction at night. This routine has given me the best of both worlds.

I utilize nonfiction in the morning for motivation and encouragement. And at night, I allow my brain to wander and experience new things with compelling fictional stories. Balancing both fiction and nonfiction has created a synergy that allows me to benefit from both differently.

I have also found that listening to self-help audiobooks in the mornings is a great way to feel empowered while getting more done. I can listen to audiobooks while driving to work, working out, or getting ready for my day. The minute I slack on listening to positive information, I can feel my natural tendency drift toward negative information.

## WE KNOW NOTHING: A GREAT PLACE TO START

In order to achieve success, we must be in a constant state of self-education. We do that through reading. Elon Musk credits his knowledge of physics and rocket science to reading a lot of books. When asked his secret to success, Warren Buffett pointed at a pile of books and said, "Read five hundred pages like this every day. That's how knowledge works. It builds up, like compound interest. All of you can do it, but I guarantee not many of you will."

Buffett gives three important principles to success with this one response. Knowledge is key, anyone can do it, and not many will. He is saying that we are all capable of reaching success through hard work and self-education. Despite the fact that education is readily available for anyone to take advantage of, not many people will. And that's because they lack the drive and determination to do what it takes. The broken have been ignored, neglected, and forgotten. Their desire to be seen and heard has formed a passion in them that can rarely be matched by the unbroken. Not many people can connect a great "why" to their self-education journey. There is no better "why" than to feel seen after years of being ignored and neglected. Despite that drive and determination, direction will be difficult without knowledge.

So, if you truly want to change your life, put in the work. Read anything you can get your hands on. Find any topic that interests you and learn about it . . . but there's a bit more to it than that.

The real key to developing the faculties of your mind in order to acquire anything you want is the wisdom to know that you know nothing, and therefore have everything to learn. Socrates felt that wisdom required humility and stated, "I am wiser than that man. Neither of us probably knows anything worthwhile; but he thinks he does when he does not, and I do not and do not think I do."

I am weary of know-it-alls who seem to always have the answer for everything. These people are not wise. They are ego-driven and merely want to win arguments or prove themselves to others. Greek philosopher Epictetus said, "It is impossible for a man to learn what he thinks he already knows." Embrace your naïveté and wear it like a badge of honor.

Obtaining this wisdom will not only help you get what you want in this life, but it will also allow you to appreciate what you have when you get it.

. . . . . . . . . . . . . . . . . . . . . . . . . . . . . . . . .

Growing up in poverty, I had no interest in art or history. I had never experienced real art or taken the time to learn about it. Then, one day, I am twenty-one years old, just married into a wealthy family, and standing in the Louvre Museum. In front of me was some of the world's most famous art like the *Mona Lisa* and the *Venus de Milo*. From there, the Eiffel Tower, and then on to Italy to see the Trevi Fountain, the Leaning Tower of Pisa, the Colosseum, and Pompeii. I was seeing places I never dreamed I would see, and most of the time, I didn't even know what country I was in. All I remember was thinking that I should appreciate these places; I should be feeling something, anything at all, for these monuments. I looked around and saw people snapping pictures and in complete awe at what they were looking at. I felt nothing. I knew nothing.

My lack of education didn't allow me to appreciate anything beyond my small world. I had never taken the time to crack a book and learn about these places. I had never studied them to learn their importance or appreciate their history. At that moment, I felt as though my world was so unbelievably small and dull. I was traveling around the world to visit the most famous places in history, and I couldn't care less.

I have very few regrets in my life. Standing in front of such beauty and history with zero appreciation for it is one of them. That trip was a strong dose of reality. It was confirmation that money would never change me. I could have expensive clothes and drive an expensive car, but without wisdom, my world would remain small.

Without knowledge and wisdom, all things fall flat. Art is not beautiful, success is not enjoyable, and money can't buy what you lack. It supports the very principles Warren Buffett was relaying: We all have the key to success at our disposal. We must choose the hard path and stop seeking quick fixes. The lottery is not the answer to your problems. More money is not the solution; wisdom is. If money is truly your motivator, wisdom will allow you to obtain it. With wisdom you will not lose it. Knowledge and wisdom will allow you to re-create success as many times as you want.

> "How much better to get wisdom than gold! To get understanding is to be chosen rather than silver."
> **–Proverbs 16:16 ES**

This approach has become my go-to response to negativity. If something makes me feel bad, I know that I need to positivity mine it until I find a solution. This makes me feel even better because I retake control of my situation. Nobody has the power or ability to make me feel bad about myself. I will take any rejection, denial, or hate and turn it into motivation. I will use attempts to bring me down as motivation to go even higher.

**With a mindset like that, people are either helping you or helping you.** However, it is a difficult mindset to apply when your feelings get crushed. Positivity mining is an effective way to quickly bypass hurt feelings and get back in the game.

## PRACTICE AND REPETITION, COURAGE AND COMMITMENT

If you want to experience the power of growth from positivity mining, you need to start practicing. You need to embrace that you are attempting to rewire your brain, and that takes time and repetition. Start mining every situation that makes you feel bad. Constantly ask yourself how to turn the negatives in your life into positives.

Hate your job? What if that job was so bad that it motivated you to find a better one? You despise your work so much that you spend all your free time finding a job you love. Suddenly, you are applying to positions you are truly passionate about. That job that you hated so much has become a catalyst for positive change. Now the job you hate has meaning. Its misery has purpose. That is a growth mindset. That is how you will start positivity mining every situation and changing your brain's neuropathways to seek success.

One thing that goes hand in hand with positivity mining is courage and commitment. When you analyze your situation and find a positive solution, having the courage to commit to that solution is vital. Many people positivity mine their situations, find a perfect solution, and are too afraid to commit.

Please understand that I am constantly afraid, and you should be, too. Fear causes us to prepare. Fear is the perfect guiding force when seeking to transition into success.

The day I graduated the Special Forces Qualification Course will forever be one of the highlights of my life. I am so proud of that day because it was so difficult to get there. I was so close to failing that course that it was by the grace of God and some good people that I passed. I was terrified to go to Special Forces selection because I knew it would be one of the most difficult things I had ever done. We already feel so fragile that we think failure will break us, when, in fact, the opposite is true. Failure is growth and helps make us strong. Everything good in our lives will be attached to fear. Everything great starts as fear. Fear that we could want something so bad and not be able to obtain it. Fear that we are not good enough. Fear that we could get what we want and lose it. It is persevering through that fear that gives everything value.

Be courageous and commit. Learn to chase your fears instead of running from them. Choose growth over victimhood.

### Broken Brains Explained

Due to our pasts, many of us broken individuals have developed physiological changes that have permanently altered the way we view the world and our places in it. It is an important step to acknowledge how our pasts have affected us so we can move forward appropriately.

According to the National Center for Biotechnology Information (NCBI), the first stage in a "cascade of events" produced by early trauma or maltreatment "involves the disruption of chemicals that function as neurotransmitters (e.g., cortisol, norepinephrine, dopamine)." This causes an escalation of the stress response, which can "negatively affect critical neural growth" during "specific sensitive periods of childhood development." The study goes on to say that this can even lead to cell death![19]

Understanding that my brain development was potentially altered due to childhood trauma was both upsetting . . . and freeing. It helped me embrace that some challenges would be more difficult for me than for others. I have struggled my entire life with social interactions. I have often found myself remorseful post conflict due to my overreactions and misconduct.

I started to lose faith in my ability to assess situations because I so frequently got it wrong. I would deem someone's actions as sinister; everything would feel like a betrayal, as though everyone were conspiring against me. Once I acknowledged that this behavior could be the result of PTSD and brain development issues, I started to pay closer attention.

I started to see patterns. I overinflated my failures and took things far more personally than everyone else. The more mistakes I made, the less I trusted my instincts.

According to research conducted by Christine Heim et al., one of the differences in childhood trauma survivors' brains is the reduction of a hormone called oxytocin, a neuropeptide linked to social behaviors. The study found that neuropeptide oxytocin, which is important for social affiliation and support, attachment, trust, and management of stress and anxiety, was "markedly decreased in the cerebrospinal fluid of women who had been exposed to childhood maltreatment, particularly those who had experienced emotional abuse."[20]

The study also said, "The more childhood traumas a person had experienced, and the longer their duration, the lower that person's current level of oxytocin was likely to be and the higher her rating of current anxiety was likely to be."

Research has found that oxytocin increases how much awareness we have of social clues, positive and negative; it also increases desire to interact with people. Childhood trauma could be reducing our levels of oxytocin and making social interactions far more difficult to accurately assess, causing social anxieties and misunderstandings.

## Chapter 10

# JOURNALING

*"A journal is your completely unaltered voice."*
**—Lucy Dacus**

A journal is a powerful tool that helps keep our goals in focus. Through the power of journaling, you will learn to become self-motivated, self-aware, and goal-oriented. Only by tracking how far you have come will you find the motivation to continue forward. The journal and the process of journaling are key to success.

People have more than six thousand thoughts per day. Researchers conducted brain imaging scans of participants while they were either resting or watching a movie. When our brains transfer from one thought to the next, they create a "thought worm" that gives off detectable brain activity. When sleep is factored in, six thousand thoughts per day translates to roughly six and a half thoughts per minute.[26]

Now think back on the last few days. What do you remember from those 24,000 thoughts? Which ones hold the most value? What lessons were there? Which of those thoughts made you emotional? Which of those thoughts inspired you? All this information is data that you need in order to make informed decisions about your future.

We can't possibly decide which of those six thousand thoughts a day are important the moment we have them. We need to develop a process for organizing and assessing these thoughts.

One day, while filming a YouTube series called *Wine and Rations*, where Navy SEAL Andy Stumpf and I pair military meals (MREs or Meals Ready to Eat) with alcoholic beverages, I got a message from someone I had looked up to since I was a private in the military: Evan Hafer from Black Rifle Coffee. He invited my crew and me out to film with him and check out his operation in Salt Lake City, Utah.

Once there, we linked up with Evan and did exactly what you think the CEO of a coffee company would do: We made coffee. Up until this point, my idea of making coffee consisted of pouring a heaping pile of grounds into a drip coffee maker and letting it fly. So I was intrigued when one of Evan's employees suddenly started a science project for a cup of joe.

I watched as she pulled out scales and science class beakers and measured everything she was working with. I asked Evan what the point of all that measuring was. He told me that in order to get the perfect cup of coffee, you needed data. You need to measure the exact amount of water and coffee grounds in order to adjust the ratio, which changes the strength and flavor of the coffee.

Instantly I realized that this approach was far more valuable than a good cup of coffee. It was the key to self-improvement. How can we make changes to our habits, thoughts, and goals when we don't track the data?

Most of us treat our lives the same way I treated coffee. Pour a bunch in and hope for the best. If we don't like it, we have no idea what changes to make. Yet if we start to measure and track the data, we can adjust the ratios and fine-tune our lives. Maybe coffee isn't important enough to do all that work for, but your future is.

This chapter highlights the importance of journaling, which is a valuable tool that will allow you to collect data on your progress and fine-tune your life. This fine-tuning will stop the guesswork and help you make progress at a faster rate. You will no longer guess which of your six thousand thoughts are worth paying attention to.

## DATA YOU CAN RELY ON

Everything about your transition to success will be smoother when you have data to rely on. One of the most feared aspects of Special Forces Assessment and Selection is land navigation. With nothing more than a compass, protractor, and map you must traverse miles of North Carolina woods in the middle of the night. People fear this phase the most because if you didn't track your data, it is nearly impossible to course correct.

Your ability to course correct will depend on the data you have collected. Before you step off, you are at a known location. It is up to you to plan a route from your current location to your desired one. It is important when planning a route to create as many checkpoints as possible. These allow you to know roughly where you are along the way. Then your only goal is to stick with that plan and keep as much data on distance and direction traveled as possible.

If you get lost, you can revert to that data in order to retrace your route. Often candidates like to skip detailed planning and choose instead to use techniques like handrailing roads. The idea is that you only need to follow alongside a road and if you do not cross it then you should only have to track distance traveled. This approach is quick and gets the candidate out moving ahead of their peers.

This approach often results in candidates getting lost and having zero data to rely on. Panic sets in, and their situation continues to deteriorate until they are hopelessly wandering around the woods.

We are the candidates in this scenario trying to navigate to a better place in life. In order to get to that place, we need a solid route plan and as much data as possible for when we lose our way.

## FINDING YOUR REAL "WHY"

I lost my way during my second deployment with Special Forces in 2016. Leadership was causing a rift within our team, and it was making our lives miserable. The following is a section of my journaling during that time.

*14 October 2016*

*Part of what makes me who I am is that I do not stop seeking new experiences. I am only thirty, too young to commit to a job forever unless that job is completely fulfilling, and this is not. I do not want to spend any more time away from home. I want to* work in Colorado and stay there until Pam and I want to move. SO, new direction.

Apply for police department, fire department, finish degree (very important, opens a lot of doors). Once a cop, try it out, try SWAT then put in an application for DEA, or stay, whatever feels right. I am tired of being under a contract.

17 October 2016

This decision seems to be passing the test of time and sleep. Sleeping on a decision has an amazing way of weeding out impulsive ideas. You will undoubtedly wake up one morning, realizing your thoughts were off and merely entertaining to contemplate. "It is the mark of an educated mind to be able to entertain a thought, without accepting it." Entertaining thoughts is how we grow. My true desire for getting out is Mia, I can't keep leaving her like this, it's not fair. She needs a father. Hopefully God has the same vision.

15 November 2016

6 days left in Gamberi, should feel like the end. However, every day on this camp feels like an eternity. This is a toxic environment BUT good side is I have a new purpose and can finally put the military behind me. I can do so while accomplishing my goals. It's been a crazy ride. Although more of it bad than good. So, it's time to call it.

That deployment was an extremely difficult time in my life. I never realized how bad Special Forces could be until I lost trust in leadership. As bad as things were at camp, none of that compared to missing my daughter. I knew I needed to make some big changes, but I was terrified.

The first thing I did was create a route plan. I would finish my bachelor's degree in order to have more employment opportunities and start applying for police and fire departments until my degree was done. With that route plan in hand, I got to work. I started waking up hours before the rest of my team to do schoolwork. I spent every free minute applying for jobs online and researching different career fields.

Those journal entries gave me a release and helped me to cope with my situation in the moment. Getting those feelings out of my head and on paper started a chain of actions. I started to accept through journaling that I needed change. I then came to realize that, despite my unhappiness with leadership, the real reason for change was to spend more time with my family. Journaling allowed me to find my real "why." Having that "why" gave me the drive to create a plan and see it through.

I started out-processing from the Army with five other guys who also decided to move on from the military. As the days counted down, each one of them got cold feet and reenlisted, despite wanting to achieve different things in their lives. Getting out of the military before retirement is scary. You are giving up a respected career, health insurance, and guaranteed pay. My journaling helped me avoid doing the same thing as the five other guys. It kept me focused, and when I got cold feet, I resorted back to my plan.

I can now look back on those journal entries knowing that I followed my plan to the letter. I finished my degree, got accepted into the police department, and served as an officer on a small team until I chose to move on. No contract was looming over my head. When I was done being a police officer, I had the freedom to walk away. I did so in order to chase my ultimate dream, something I didn't know if I would ever do: follow in my grandfather's footsteps and start my own business.

## HOW I JOURNAL

I utilize journaling in a variety of ways. First, I use it to track my goals and give myself accountability. If I write it down, then it's important, and at some point, I will look back on my journals and must answer for why I did, or did not, pursue that important goal. Secondly, I write about emotional instances in my life in order to better understand them. My first book, *Rising Above*, was essentially one long journal entry that aided in my recovery.

Digging into my past and writing it down allowed me to face instances that were having a lingering effect on my life—most of which I had been suppressing for so many years that I didn't realize they were still affecting me. It was through the process of journaling my life and eventually turning it into a book that I realized how many benefits came from my past.

The more I dug, the more I could connect positive aspects of my personality and character to struggles in my childhood. That revelation led me to writing this book, to empower the broken and help them make the same connections. Once we understand where our power is derived from, we can hone it and use it more effectively.

## THE SCIENCE OF WRITING

Researchers have found journaling to be so powerful that it can help speed up physical recovery in patients undergoing a medically necessary biopsy. "We think writing about distressing events helped participants make sense of the events and reduce distress," says Elizabeth Broadbent, a professor of medicine at the University of Auckland in New Zealand.[27]

Studies revealed that writing about stressful events can reduce hormones such as cortisol, which then improves sleep. Cortisol is a steroid hormone produced by the adrenal glands.[28] It is released into the bloodstream to alter the body during fight or flight scenarios. This is a perfectly normal and healthy response to increase chances of survival. However, if you have had a past full of trauma and abuse, you could be stuck in a constant state of fight or flight. This overabundance of cortisol puts you at an increased risk for anxiety, depression, digestive problems, sleep problems, weight gain, and more.

The ability to reduce cortisol and improve sleep can be life-changing for people suffering from anxiety disorders and PTSD. Dr. James Pennebaker, a psychologist and leading expert in the field of expressive writing, wrote, "We know from multiple studies that there are enhancements in immune function, drops in blood pressure, improvements in sleep, and drops in other markers of stress. People go to the doctor less in the months after expressive writing. Other studies find faster wound healing, greater mobility among people with arthritis, and the list goes on."[29]

## JOURNALING FOR THE BROKEN

Journaling isn't just a good idea for the broken; it is necessary. We live with so much anxiety and stress. Those of us suffering from PTSD are dealing with intrusive thoughts, flashbacks, anxiety, feelings of impending doom . . . the list feels endless. The idea that putting pen to paper can physically and emotionally heal us is remarkable.

So many people are self-medicating with drugs and alcohol, and we are losing greatness daily. Those people, like me, were likely never taught that they had tools at their disposal to reduce stress and anxiety without prescriptions or booze. I have seen so many soldiers survive combat only to come home and take their own lives. People are hurting, and that pain is meaningful. It needs to be written down and evaluated. **We need to understand our pain so we can extract as much growth and positivity from it as possible.**

### Staying Positive

Staying positive about our lives and our futures can be difficult. One way to help us keep a positive outlook is by being grateful for what we have. According to UCLA's Mindfulness Awareness Research Center, having a grateful attitude changes the molecular structure of the brain, keeps the gray matter functioning, and makes us healthier and happier.[30]

It may seem there is always something negative about our environments that we are working to change. That does not mean we should solely focus on the negative. There is always something to be grateful for. Your health, your family's health, enough food to eat, loved ones . . . there is always something going right in your life. Giving yourself a couple minutes a day to be grateful for those things can have a compounding effect of positive change, and a great way to do that is to incorporate a gratitude journal into your daily writing. It's easy: simply write three things you are grateful for every day.

It would seem that writing down your feelings would be an easy task. Yet, it can be counterintuitive to be open and honest about our emotions. I have found that not sticking to any style or approach can be helpful. I journal however I feel in that moment. I allow my emotional state to dictate the type of journal entry I make. If I am feeling strong and confident, I may list my goals in order. If I feel lost and in need of direction, I will write down a question and contemplate it.

The question may be *What do I want?* or *What am I missing?* Then I spend time with the question and write down anything that feels important. When I am feeling stressed about things outside of my control, for example, whether Netflix would pick me to be a host or if there was an open spot on the SWAT team, I create a chart. One side is a list of goals that are in my control. The other side are goals that I have no control over. This allows me to refocus the energy wasted on things not in my control toward the things that are.

One of the best parts about journaling is the ability to go back through a month or even a year of your life and see what took place. The ability to see your emotional journey unfold is so empowering and inspiring. We often forget the struggles we have faced to get where we are. Life is difficult, it is scary, and at times, it is unbelievably painful. Yet we find ways to get through those times and keep moving forward.

Our journals give us the ability see what fears and insecurities we were dealing with. I often laugh at the amount of fear and anxiety I had toward an event that in hindsight was so insignificant. Journals allow us to revisit hard situations and see what we did right and how things worked themselves out. In that moment, you may have thought everything was on the line, but now you can look back and know that you overreacted, and maybe you don't have to overreact next time. Our lives are full of valuable lessons, yet without proper documentation we will forget those lessons, causing us to relive them.

· · · · · · · · · · · · · · · · · · · · · · · · · · · · ·

We are like Special Forces candidates walking through the woods at night. When we get lost or want to make sure we are headed in the right direction, we look to our past. We use the data collected along the way to know exactly where we are, and then determine where we want to be. Without this data, we will inevitably find ourselves wandering without direction. Like drifters, we will just hope we stumble upon something better. If you have been drifting, maybe it is time to start tracking your progress and keeping a journal. Maybe it is time to start collecting data on yourself so you can fine-tune your thoughts and actions.

Not everyone needs to make their morning cup of coffee like an eighth-grade science experiment. However, everyone needs to treat their lives like one: tracking every detail, taking notes, keeping logs, looking back at what worked and what did not . . . figuring out who we are and where our strengths come from. When we know that much about ourselves, there is nothing that can stop us. We will not get lost because we can easily check our data, course correct, and find our way.

## Chapter 11

# THE CONFIDENCE OF A FIT BODY

"Perhaps happiness is always to be found in the journey uphill, and not in the fleeting sense of satisfaction awaiting at the next peak."
**—Jordan Peterson**

Not having a father around, I usually ended up avoiding most things other boys did. I avoided them out of fear of being ridiculed. I didn't know how to throw a baseball properly, I couldn't spiral a football, and I certainly didn't know how to lift weights. Until one day in middle school when our teacher brought us to the weight room.

The football coach was there teaching the players how to lift weights. He taught them that lifting weights builds character. He told them that anyone had access to the gym, and nobody had an excuse to not work out. He was teaching them that the gym was a place to test themselves and outwork other people.

I felt inspired by his speech and watched carefully as he demonstrated proper form when bench-pressing and deadlifting. Then he walked them around the gym to each workout station and showed them how to use the machines. He was teaching them gym etiquette, such as to always put the weights back when you were done, don't linger on machines, and never drop the weights.

However, I was picking up on a different message. I didn't need money or a ride to practice in order to work out. *What if fitness was my sport since I couldn't afford to play football or baseball?* I thought.

Here was an activity I could do for free, and I could do it by myself. If I got to school early, I could go to the gym. And just like that, I had a sport . . . one that did not require sign-up fees, tryouts, rides, or even skill for that matter. I could take the time to learn this sport and become good at it at my own pace. As I started to become fitter, I learned something very important: there was a power derived from confidence that transcended social class. And the middle school weight room was where I learned to harness that power.

Broken people start life at a deficit, and we need every advantage possible to reach baseline and work toward success. Being fitter than the day before is something that is desired by every person on the planet. It doesn't matter if you are dead broke or a billionaire, everyone wants to be fit. But not many people are willing to put in the work to get there. That presents an opportunity for us to level the playing field.

## THE STRESS INOCULATOR

Research suggests that while exercise initially spikes stress responses in the body, it reduces levels of stress hormones like epinephrine and cortisol after long bouts.[31] These findings were enhanced when the physical activity involved competition. Biologically, exercise is a form of stress inoculation. So not only is fitness providing us with the confidence of a fit body, but it is also allowing us to practice managing stress in a positive way. That is a game changer for people who have been stuck in a constant state of fight or flight as a result of trauma.

According to Wendy Suzuki, neuroscientist and professor of neural science and psychology, fitness decreases feelings of anxiety, improves focus and concentration, promotes growth of new brain cells, and protects your brain from aging and neurodegenerative diseases.[32] Let's not forget the list of physical benefits like reduced risk of disease, strengthening bones and muscles, weight management... the list goes on. So, with all the overwhelming benefits, why are people choosing to ignore such an obvious advantage?

I believe the reason is partly due to people's misconception that you must *look* fit in order to extract the confidence from working out. The goal is to be in a constant state of self-improvement mentally and physically. When you combine these two, you will increase your chances of success and decrease your transition period. You will be more willing to take risks and face failure. You will realize that confidence comes from your willingness to put in the work, which takes the power away from others and puts it back in your hands.

So many people avoid starting because they don't see themselves reaching the highest level. Why read when I will never be as smart as

Jordan Peterson? Why lift weights when I will never look like Chris Hemsworth? This all-or-nothing mentality prevents many from experiencing the benefits firsthand.

## YOU DON'T NEED 10,000 HOURS

In one of my favorite books, *Outliers,* Malcolm Gladwell talks about the "10,000-hour rule." Gladwell asserts that the key to becoming an expert in any given skill requires ten thousand hours of practice. Although I agree with Gladwell, it is important to understand that we do not need to be experts in everything that brings us value. I will never be a fitness "expert." I have used physical fitness to become a Green Beret, a police officer, and to run ultra-marathons. Yet, I fully understand that I have no need to become an "expert," and neither do you.

This idea that we must master a task or avoid it is a detriment to our personal growth. Jim Collins, in his book *Good to Great*, writes that "good is the enemy of great." Now, I am not disagreeing with Jim Collins here; however, it is important to understand that in order to be great at one thing, we need to be good at a multitude of other things. Things like journaling, finances, physical fitness, and self-education.

Physical fitness is about the journey uphill. The struggle itself is precisely where the benefit is derived. If you have been on the edge of starting a new sport, or signing up for a fitness class, stop waiting to get involved. You will start reaping the reward of confidence from the minute you overcome your fear and walk in the door.

## THE POWER OF GROWTH STEMS FROM THE JOURNEY

When I was a police officer, one of my favorite times of the year was when new recruits graduated from the academy. It was hilarious to watch them walk in to roll call for the first time completely lost. Like clockwork they would find a seat in the back of the room, trying to avoid detection. Unbeknownst to them, their attempts to fly under the radar put them directly in the spotlight. In roll call, senior officers sat in the back and new recruits were saved seats directly in front of the sergeant.

We would joke about which old man was about to lose his mind when he showed up and saw someone in his seat. The awkward interaction between the vet and the rookie would inspire everyone to hone in on the recruit. It would get them nice and nervous before they were asked to do the one thing people hated most: public speaking. They were instructed to introduce themselves and tell everyone why they wanted to be cops. Our goal was always twofold during those interactions: first, to have fun, and second, to start the stress inoculation process in a safe environment. It wouldn't take long before these rookies would be on their own having to make real-world decisions. Just like in Special Operations, the best way to deal with stress is through practice.

Then one day, a 5'8", 200-plus-pound recruit walked in. His shoulders were pulled back, he looked everyone in the eye, and his introduction was flawless. I sat there wondering where his confidence was coming from. Here he was, clearly overweight with no prior law enforcement experience, and he walked in like he'd been there for a decade.

I could tell he was not arrogant, just supremely confident in himself. He was polite and seemed very humble. He demanded respect from people, and they gave it instantly. I don't believe anyone else thought any more about it. They just accepted that he deserved more respect than the other recruits. They likely chalked it up to a gut feeling about him. I was intrigued, because I know the work required to have that type of confidence. Personally, I had to maintain a high standard of physical fitness. I worked hard journaling, reading, and obtaining degrees, all so I could walk into any room with *that* type of confidence.

A couple of weeks later, I was in the police station gym working out before roll call. The recruit walked in with some boxing gloves and focus mitts. He saw that I had some gloves on the bench and had been doing some bag work. He asked if I wanted to hit the mitts for a couple minutes. At the time I was training in Brazilian Jiu-Jitsu (BJJ) and striking at one of the best gyms in Colorado, High Altitude Martial Arts. One thing I learned early was that being good with focus mitts is no easy skill.

The recruit started calling out strikes and pushing me to hit harder and move faster. "Come on, man, you got more than that!" he yelled. Within ten minutes, my arms felt like wet noodles. He had given me a master class in striking.

Turns out, he had come from a rough background and was raised in poverty in the Denver projects. He was a former boxer and now coached at The Brotherhood, a police officer–run youth boxing gym designed to help kids get off the streets. This guy may have looked overweight, but he had lost nearly a hundred pounds to get back in fighting shape and pursue his dream of being a police officer.

This recruit was the perfect example that the power of growth stems from the journey, not the destination. This recruit didn't look fit. He didn't have a square jaw or a six-foot frame. He looked unassuming and kind of sloppy. Yet when he walked into a room, he owned it. His confidence was contagious and inspiring to be around. I hit mitts with him every chance I could. Nobody worked harder in the station than him. There is power in progress.

## AND THERE IS NO FINISH LINE

It is important to realize that progress is the only thing that matters. There is no finish line; there is no such thing as mastery. You are either progressing or you are not. That can be an amazing revelation, because once you understand that mastery is irrelevant, starting now is the same as starting twenty years ago. You are not behind. It is never too late. And there are only two measurements for growth: progress or no progress.

Nothing demonstrates this point better than the art of Brazilian Jiu-Jitsu. People often assume that the ranking structure of the belt is a hierarchy within the gym. In some gyms, it may feel that way; however, the belt is merely to identify skill levels for live sparring.

The white belt leaves with the same benefits as the black belt. The person who walks into class on day one to learn mount or side control is immediately on the same path as the black belt learning advanced techniques. There is a saying in BJJ: "A black belt is a white belt who never quit." **Martial arts teaches us that there is no destination.** We extract the benefits from training every time we step on the mats. People may think that BJJ practitioners train solely for the fighting skills; however, the real benefit is the feeling and confidence derived from progress.

My progress gives me confidence that I carry into every other aspect of my life. Once you start your fitness journey, whether it is in a weight room, on the mats, or both, you will immediately access the power of progress and will be able to use that confidence toward achieving your goals.

## Find an Activity That Turns Off Your Brain

I can't emphasize enough the importance of finding a physical activity that focuses your attention. I am still not sure if my brain ever stops working as a side effect of childhood trauma, war, or just being born that way. Whatever the reason, an overactive brain can be mentally and physically exhausting. When I run, I think; when I lift, I think. When I am with my family, my mind will veer off without realizing it.

I have learned to harness my thoughts and use them to create products, solve problems, find solutions, and many other positive things. However, I struggle greatly getting my thoughts to shut off or even to slow down.

I have watched so many high achievers turn to alcohol for this very reason, myself included. I have lost more friends and fellow operators from suicide at this point than I have in combat. I want you to know that if you are struggling and think alcohol is the answer, you are not alone. I have learned over the years that alcohol only makes it worse, and the best solution I have found is Brazilian Jiu-Jitsu. You cannot think about work, life, stress, or anxiety when someone is trying to choke you out.

For that hour and a half, I get physically exhausted, which helps decrease anxiety and stress, but more importantly, I get a mental break from my busy mind. I encourage you to find an activity that requires all your attention. Alcohol may feel like it is having a relaxing effect. However, I have found that it leads to darker thought patterns that quickly become depressing.

The act of competing with another person is fulfilling in ways that are unmatched by solo activity. If you find yourself working out and still struggling to find an emotional and physical release, a competitive sport may be the answer. That terrifying pressure of performing in front of others will soon become your fuel. Just know that alcohol is not the escape you are looking for. That route will often lead to the unraveling of nearly every improvement you have made.

### The Confidence We Need

It is important to understand the damaging effect trauma has on our self-esteem so we can work toward correcting it. In 2018, a study was conducted with 350 Japanese college students to determine the relationship between PTSD and self-esteem. The researchers concluded there was a positive correlation between total PTSD scores and self-esteem scores. The higher the tendency for PTSD, the lower the self-esteem.[33]

The researchers believe that "the onset of PTSD causes a decline in memory ability and attentional function, which interferes with one's life and leads to self-denial, resulting in a decline in self-esteem among those with a high tendency for PTSD."

We know that children develop a strong sense of self during their formative years. Many of us were neglected and abused during those years. Maybe we blamed ourselves for the way we were treated. Maybe we assumed that it was our fault or that we didn't deserve the life we saw others living. Whatever the reason, we often feel like we are not good enough.

And when things do go right in our lives, we find ourselves dealing with imposter syndrome, which is the feeling of being a fraud or unworthy of our own achievements.

**It is up to us to combat these feelings by infusing confidence into our lives.** According to clinical psychologist Barbara Markway, PhD, confidence reduces fear and anxiety by giving us the ability to quiet our inner critic and stop ruminating or mulling over worries and perceived mistakes. Confidence increases our resilience by giving us coping mechanisms for setbacks and failures. It improves our relationships by allowing us to focus less on ourselves and more on our partners. Lastly, Dr. Markway suggests that confidence strengthens our sense of authentic self, allowing us to accept our weaknesses and prevent them from changing our self-worth.[34]

**Everyone needs confidence to succeed, but the broken need it to survive.** We need confidence like we need water. We need it to stop ruminating over our perceived mistakes and start living our lives to the fullest.

Developing self-confidence will allow you to take the required risks to achieve success. Confidence will help you push through self-doubt and fear. It will allow you to trust your instincts and face your failures. Confidence is a tactical advantage that you need to harness for the rest of your life. **We do that by taking care of ourselves mentally and physically.** We do what Jordan Peterson recommends in his book *12 Rules for Life* and **treat ourselves like someone we are responsible for helping**.

## Chapter 12

# ONE THING AT A TIME

"Things don't matter equally. Success is found in doing what matters most."
**—Gary Keller**

Training to become Special Forces was one of the hardest things I had ever done. Despite how difficult the overall process was, there were certain moments that stood out. These moments nearly broke me mentally and physically. These were the moments that helped me develop mental tactics that I would later use to survive gunfights, city riots, and multiple career changes.

It is likely that many of the broken have already developed some of these mental tactics and used them to survive their trauma. Yet it can be difficult to transition those tactics from trauma to success because we have disassociated from our pasts, leaving behind not only the memories and pain, but also the lessons we could have learned from the experiences.

## PUSHED PAST MY LIMITS

These are some of the moments that pushed me past my limits, and taught me how to avoid letting my greatest strength, my mind, become my greatest weakness. The first was an event in Special Forces Assessment and Selection (SFAS) that had my mind begging me to quit with every step.

The teams were tasked to find the "downed pilot" and rig a hasty litter to recover him from the crash site. We were given a map and a location of the pilot and his downed aircraft. First, we had to find him and then move him an undisclosed number of miles back to safety. We arrived at the location to find a pile of equipment on the ground. There were some lashings, four large six- to eight-foot steel poles, and a giant sandbag representing our "pilot." We had to turn this mass of steel and sandbag into something we could carry for long distances.

With rucks on our backs already weighing forty-five to fifty pounds, we quickly lashed the poles together and attached the sandbag the best we could. The final apparatus was a poorly tied monstrosity with dead weight hanging from the center. From there, we tried to fit as many men under the apparatus as possible to share the load. We found out that our rucksacks prevented too many people from carrying the weight at a time. So instead, we decided to have alternates and switch at regular intervals to give people breaks.

When it was my turn, I ran under the pole and lifted it off my teammate's back with my ruck frame. That allowed my teammate to slide off the apparatus and "rest." The minute I took over the apparatus for the first time, shock ran through my body. I had severely underestimated how heavy this thing was. It felt like it was twisting and compressing my spine. My mind started screaming for me to stop and throw in the towel. Every step, the sandbag would swing from one side to the other, creating even more energy that had to be countered in order to move forward.

I started to feel my hip bones pulling from their sockets with every step. I was waiting to hear a snap or a pop as my joints would eventually fail under the load. My mind kept punishing me with the idea that I was pushing myself too far. It was trying to convince me that I was doing permanent damage, and I needed to stop.

It was like a voice growing louder and louder until all I could think about was quitting. Then I looked up and saw that we were about to ascend a steep sand hill. That was the last thing I wanted to see. Up until that point, we were walking on a flat dirt road, and it was already agony. The sight of that sand hill made me feel sick to my stomach.

I decided in that moment that I couldn't do it. My body could not physically make it up that hill without breaking. I decided to quit, and since I was going to quit anyway, I put the hill out of my mind. Instead of looking at it, I looked straight down at my feet. I put all my energy into each step. That way, after I quit, I could still walk. My right foot would hit the ground, and all I focused on was making sure my hip didn't pop out. Once I got through a full stride with my right foot, I had to refocus that energy to the left foot.

Suddenly, I found myself lost in thought, visualizing each step and the function of my hip inside the joint socket. I visualized the movement of the joint and the tendons surrounding it. It felt like I could see into my leg and identify tendons and muscles through the sharp pings of pain that pulsated throughout. Suddenly I realized that my intense focus had subdued the pain for countless steps. I looked up to discover that we had just crested the hill. I managed to forget about the hill and focus on one step at a time.

Another time I reached my mental limits was in the Special Forces Qualification Course. It was during one of the hardest phases of the course called Small Unit Tactics (SUT). This is where you learn to master basic infantry tactics. We do this by running battle drills sometimes for twenty-four hours straight. A Green Beret masters the basics, and this allows us to teach these lessons to foreign militaries regardless of their skill level. If we can get them good at the basics, we can operate cohesively, and more importantly, they can operate independently once we leave.

It was the final mission of the course, and all we had to do was maneuver to an overwatch position and wait for another team to initiate an ambush. Once the ambush was initiated on the target location, we would link up with the other team, clear the target to the limit of advance (LOA), and we would be done with SUT. It would have been the best spot to be in if it weren't for the freezing temperatures and the intermittent freezing rain.

I lay on the ground in a prone position with every ounce of heat being sucked out of my body. We had nothing to do but lay in this position and stay awake until sunrise when the attack would be initiated. It must have been six to eight hours before sunrise. I lay there with nothing else to do but think about how cold I was. My mind started the same pattern of focusing on how many hours were left in the night. Then I would feel the biting wind cut through my uniform and bring a chill to my body that felt like knives cutting me to the bone.

I thought about how there was no way I could lie there freezing for another six hours. I couldn't believe I was having this thought of wanting to give up. By this time in the course, I knew I didn't have quit in me. I had enough situations compounded to know that I can always push one more step or make it one more minute. Yet here was this internal chatter back in full force trying to convince me that what lay ahead was too much to bear.

I reminded myself of the downed sandbag pilot and how I needed to focus on the here and now. I needed to put the hours I had left out of my head and try to make this very moment as bearable as possible. Downed pilot taught me that if I gave every ounce of energy to getting through that very moment, at some point I will have distracted myself until there are no more moments left. I started to think about every piece of equipment in my rucksack.

I reached into my ruck and pulled out extra socks and T-shirts, shoving them down the front of my pants. Anything that could act as a barrier between myself and the heat-sucking ground. Every time I added something new to the inside of my pants or top, I felt a small victory. Just the act of improving my situation made me feel better. Knowing that I did something about my suffering besides feeling sorry for myself encouraged me to make it a little longer.

I continued to play this game for hours. Shove something in my pants, pretend it was working for as long as possible. Once the cold became unbearable again, start looking for something else. Finally, the night sky began to change. It wasn't much, but I could see a light blue haze break the darkness. It was finally happening! The sun was finally working its way back to our side of Earth. Despite having a couple more hours before sunrise, that little bit of hope was all I needed.

The sun finally rose and we began packing our stuff and preparing for the assault. It wasn't until we did that I realized my feet were completely numb. As we descended the hill toward the objective, I was stumbling. We broke the tree line and the sun lit up my face and a blanket of warmth covered my entire body. That night had been one of the hardest nights of my life, yet that morning was one of the happiest. Not only did we make it to feel the warmth of the sun, but we were also done with SUT. That numb-footed walk was a victory walk, and we had earned every minute of it.

· · · · · · · · · · · · · · · · · · · · · · · · · · · · · · · · ·

I tell these stories to highlight the mind's ability to turn on us when we are pushing past our limits. To the mind, that limit is there for a reason. It is a safety boundary that prevents us from having to face the unknown. Every time you push that boundary, your mind accepts the new limits as part of that safe zone. Being Special Forces teaches operators to become comfortable with this pattern and comfortable outside of their limits.

Operators feel fear—we will never rid ourselves of fear—however, we become so familiar with the pattern that we can ignore our mind's plea to stop and turn back. **We do this by narrowing our focus from the overall mission to the very next step.**

I wanted to know if there was any research that supported this mental tactic. So, I reached out to a friend and colleague, Sean Burkhart, who is a chiropractic physician and functional neurologist. He replied:

> *During stress, your body releases epinephrine and adrenaline. These hormones modify your visual field by narrowing it, creating tunnel-like focus, and increasing your concentration. A study on elite and recreational runners evaluated how visual attention can increase*

*performance—demonstrating that this strategy can work at all competitive and physical fitness levels.*[35] *Controlling your focus and attention through vision can positively impact your performance and motivation.*

*The question begs, do you view stress as enhancing or debilitating? The current research inquires whether mindsets are beneficial in austere environments of extreme physical and mental stress. After following Navy SEAL candidates during BUDs, basic underwater demolition SEAL training, those with stress-IS-enhancing mindsets showed more remarkable persistence through training, faster obstacle course times, and fewer negative evaluations from peers and instructors.*[36] *The opposite was also discovered with failure-IS-enhancing candidates' success and non-limited willpower mindsets prompting negative evaluations from others. Learning to control and shift your focus can positively affect your mindset, increase your performance, and give you the mental advantage to complete each evolution.*

## THE LIMITS OF WILLPOWER

Now that we know what the brain is capable of in extreme cases like SFAS, BUDs, and the Qualification Course, how do we apply that to everyday life and success? It is important to understand that when implementing the changes recommended in this book, you will start to achieve greatness. With greatness comes roles and responsibilities that can become overwhelming. You will want to take more risks in life with your increased confidence and focus. With increased risk, it becomes easy to get overwhelmed.

For example, when I decided to turn my journal into a book, I was completely lost. I had no idea how to turn a journal into a manuscript. I didn't know anything about editing, cover design, marketing . . . I was completely overwhelmed. This left me debating whether I should even pursue something that seemed so far beyond my capabilities.

All this pushed my boundaries and sent me outside of my comfort zone. Because I was failing to narrow my focus, my mind was telling me that the unknown was too much. How could I pursue a goal when I didn't know how to do 95 percent of what it required? I doubted my progress, my direction, and my willingness to pursue the things I valued. Then I discovered a book called *The ONE Thing* by Gary Keller.[37]

The book taught me two important concepts that allowed me to transition the Special Forces mindset to everyday tasks. First, willpower was limited and needed to be utilized effectively and efficiently.

Keller wrote that willpower is depleted when "we make decisions to focus our attention, suppress our feelings and impulses, or modify our behavior in pursuit of goals." He compared it to poking a hole in a gas line. "Before long, we have willpower leaking everywhere and none left to do our most important work." His conclusion was that, like other vital resources, "willpower must be managed."

I was depleting my willpower by overwhelming myself with tasks required to reach my goal and author my first book. This technique had worked for me so many times in the past, but that was overcoming physical pain. Gary Keller's lessons taught me how to narrow my focus in a civilian setting by directing that willpower to the most important tasks.

# PRIORITIZE

The second concept was to think of tasks like a row of dominoes. When you knock over the first domino, it often causes a chain reaction. That means many of our concerns would become irrelevant by focusing on the task before.

I decided to put these lessons in action and first prioritize my task list. Once I did that, I realized that cover design, editing, marketing, website design, and so on were all useless without a finished manuscript. I had my first step to focus on, and the rest would have to wait.

I put all my energy into the most important task and that task only. Once I did that, I found a new sense of confidence in my book. I had put so much energy into the manuscript that I started to feel like it could really help people. I was also managing my willpower, and it was paying off. Once I had completed the book, it was time to figure out the next most important step. I contacted a self-publishing service with a completed manuscript in hand.

They told me that for an uncomfortably large fee they would take care of everything I was worried about. Gary Keller's advice proved effective. I knocked down one domino at a time, focusing solely on the next step. That domino created a chain reaction and moved me further along the process than I thought possible. That is when I realized that with a few tweaks, the one-foot-in-front-of-the-other mentality used in Special Operations can be just as effective in the civilian world.

## THE BACKWARDS PLAN

We so easily become overwhelmed with the things we don't know how to do. We want to achieve greatness, but with greatness comes a lot of unknowns. We must find a way to manage those unknowns and be willing to live outside of our comfort zones. We must learn to manage our willpower and focus on one thing at a time. When we take that approach and focus all our energy on one task, we eliminate so much worry and self-doubt.

Before I understood that concept, I was a nervous wreck trying to manage everything at once, always trying to find all the answers before getting into a project or attacking a goal. Now, I don't concern myself with the entire process; all that matters is that I know the most important step and focus all my energy on that step. The rest will either work itself out or become the one thing down the road.

In Special Forces, it is easy to focus on what matters most because that one thing can kill you. I never had to think about redirecting my focus on the bad guys when the 7.62 rounds were punching into the wall behind me. I didn't have to think about finding cover as I watched enemy rounds splashing in the dirt getting closer and closer. Or when my interpreter was shot standing next to me, the one thing seemed blatantly obvious: find cover. Once I found cover, the new most important thing became obvious—stop the bleeding or shoot back.

Yet when I transitioned into the civilian world, that one thing seemed to elude me. The one thing was never as obvious anymore. **Everything seemed to hold the same level of importance and it was burning me out mentally and physically.**

What really helped was getting out my journal and writing my "why." This helped me identify the true purpose of my goal and analyze what success would be for that goal. Once I had a clear idea of what success would look like, I would backwards plan. Backwards planning is a great tactic for people who struggle to get started or who get caught up in the tasks required to complete a goal.

When you start with the goal in mind, you get a feeling of excitement and motivation to see it come to fruition. It is important that you do your best to fully visualize your goal in as much detail as possible. The more real you make your goal, the more motivation you will have to see it through. With that beautifully painted end state in your mind, start working backwards, identifying steps required along the way. It is important to not worry about whether you know how to complete those steps. You are simply creating a map from one point to the other with as many checkpoints as possible.

Once you have your map created, it is time to get to work on the very first step, even if there are tons of steps along way you don't know how to tackle. Put those steps out of your mind—by the time you get to them, they will have either resolved themselves or will be the only thing to focus on.

## SEEK OUT OTHERS

Once you get to a step that you are completely lost on, it is important to remind yourself that you are not the first person to do it. There have been hundreds, if not thousands, of people before you who have accomplished that task.

Seek those people out; use them as mentors. Some of them may have written books or been on podcasts. You may be able to just contact them via Instagram or Facebook and ask. Whenever I get stumped, I search out someone who has already done it and learn everything I can. From there I either learn how to do the task myself or I find someone who can help me.

I am in that situation as I write this. I realized that I have never had the perfect pair of military boots. So, my company decided that it would be amazing to create our own. I had no idea how that process begins or even what the first step would be. The first thing I had to do was find someone who did. I got on the internet and searched companies with similar goals until I found a talented boot designer. I just reached out to him on LinkedIn and asked for help.

He replied that he couldn't help us but had a friend who could. That friend helped us design the best military boot ever made for Special Forces candidates.

Even as the boot prototype is being perfected, I have no idea how I will come up with the capital to purchase thousands of pairs. I need to ignore that step and understand that when the time comes, I will dedicate all my attention to completing it. Once we truly dedicate our attention to a task, it becomes infinitely easier to figure out. Too often we allow our attention to become diluted with too many tasks. Then it becomes difficult to formulate solutions for even the simplest of problems. How many times have you been so overwhelmed by a task that you give up on your goal?

# FEAR

Fear is a strange emotion that can overwhelm us and prevent us from achieving our goals. War taught me that fear is always going to be there, and the important thing is learning to manage it. We do that by understanding why it exists in the first place.

The things that truly matter to us are the things that scare us the most. Fear is derived from the possibility of not obtaining that which we want so desperately. The more we want something, the scarier it becomes to try, because we could fail. If we don't learn to focus our minds and harness our willpower, we could miss out on our dreams. It is easy to become overwhelmed by the steps required for greatness, yet if we just focus on one thing at a time, we will find that we can manage anything.

Learn to embrace fear as a good thing. It means that you care about what you are doing. It means that you are widening your comfort zone. Use fear as a guiding star. The minute you become comfortable and stop feeling it, seek it out. Find the things that mean so much to you they scare you to even try. Spend as much time in that state as possible. That is how you will develop your greatness.

## Chapter 13

# ON GOALS AND FAILURE

"The difference between average people and achieving people is their perception of and response to . . . failure."
**–John C. Maxwell**

I believe that we must change our perceptions of what growth means, what goals are, and what the very meaning of failure is. It goes back to how our brains are wired differently (see pages 94–96) and to how we need to work harder and smarter to get ourselves to the baseline most others take for granted.

When I decided to evaluate what I truly wanted out of life, I found that **growth was the most important thing I could pursue—growth from as many angles as possible, including mental, emotional, physical, and spiritual**. The process of becoming better is literally the only thing that brings joy and fullness into our lives. It is the only thing that matters, and I find no greater satisfaction than being slightly better today than I was yesterday.

I also realized that **goals themselves are valuable only in that they give us a reason to move forward**. Special Forces, police officer, author, master's degree . . . these were just goals I was successful in achieving. I have had just as many failed aspirations. I wanted to be a Ranger (failed selection due to injury), get on the SWAT team (failed to obtain a spot), get chosen for the Secret Service CAT team (failed hiring process), be an Air Force Special Tactics Officer (failed the math test by one point).

The more I looked at this list, the more obvious it became. **Goals are just fuel to keep us moving.** And every goal that does so is equal, whether it was achieved or not. Goals are merely circumstantial motivators to keep us focused on becoming better versions of ourselves.

I know this is true because every time I moved from one career to another, my previous goals didn't matter anymore. Yet in the moment, that goal meant everything to me. We stake our reputations, our self-worth, our value on these goals. These goals lose all meaning simply by us changing career fields.

My current goal is to become a successful business owner. It feels as though there is nothing more important than that goal. If I hadn't been in this situation so many times before, I might make the mistake of thinking that this goal matters. I might start to feel as though being a successful business owner could become my identity, or that it could define me as a person or make me feel successful.

Fortunately, I have enough experience to know that none of those things are true. This goal, like my previous goals, is valuable only because it propels me forward. It gives me motivation to get out of bed and work hard toward something meaningful. I will only feel successful when I adopt a growth mindset and focus on becoming incrementally better each day.

If you do not make this mindset shift, you will fall into the same obsessive traps as I did, trying to fill a void with achievements. You will attempt to prove yourself to others through plaques, awards, and promotions. You will find yourself never enjoying life because you think everything you want is at the next mountain peak, only to arrive and feel the same. So many of us do it. We achieve a goal, and within days we start plotting out the next one. We become stuck in a cycle of hoping the next achievement will change our self-appreciation and self-worth. We need to realize that movement is what matters—the goal is just a direction in which to do so. American novelist Henry Miller said, "One's destination is never a place but rather a new way of looking at things."[38]

Knowing that some pinnacle moment isn't coming allows us to enjoy the here and now. We can transition our focus from the future to the present. We can learn to enjoy the process and embrace the blessings of life. **Don't leave behind the confines of abuse and poverty only to trap yourself in unquenchable desire.**

Now that we have accepted that peaks do not exist, we can focus on growth itself, meaning once we are in it, we are there. Our goal is to remain there for as much of our lives as possible.

## NO PEAKS, NO FAILURE

There is no looming failure, because there is no peak to be lost. This can be a difficult concept to embrace because we want to believe that certain achievements will change how we feel about ourselves. We are so driven by what that peak will provide that it can be disheartening to hear that there is nothing there.

Understand that growth comes from the small habits used to obtain the goal and not the goal itself. Growth is that feeling you are searching for . . . being better than you were yesterday.

That is where the power of failure comes in. We learn far more from our failure than we do success. I have wasted years of my life thinking a new accomplishment would make me feel better about myself or make me impressive in the eyes of others. If you approach goals this way, you will be disappointed when you achieve them and find none of that to be true.

If your sights are set on growth and becoming the best possible version of yourself **then you will understand that failure is your best mentor**.

I look back on failed goals and opportunities and am happy about all of them. I learned so much from each loss, and then I was able to redirect that growth toward even harder goals. Each time I failed, I ended up with a more desirable outcome. When I failed Ranger selection, I used the lessons learned to become a Green Beret. With every failed attempt, I became more efficient, wiser, and more capable.

In his book *Failing Forward*, John C. Maxwell said, "The more you do, the more you fail. The more you fail, the more you learn. The more you learn, the better you get."

You must learn how to fail with grace and appreciate the experience. Those who cannot recognize failure as an opportunity will quit. Failure teaches, success confirms, quitting ends.

# LEARNING TO FAIL

So how do we learn to fail? How do we start embracing failure and extracting lessons from it? First, let's be very clear about failure and whether extracting lessons from it prevents it from hurting. It does not. There is no way around it. When you want something badly enough to pursue it, you give it everything you have, and you still fail, it hurts. Anyone who tells you that failing doesn't sting is lying. However, **there is a difference between feeling the sting and allowing that sting to destroy you**.

The first thing you do when trying to recover from failure is allow it to sting. Allow your feelings to be hurt. Grab your journal and start writing about it. Write down why it hurt, what you were hoping to get out of the achievement, and what you feel you have lost from not obtaining it. The more open you are with yourself in this phase, the easier it will be to extract the lessons. This is your chance to discover why you were so attached to this goal.

Dig in while the moment is fresh and start connecting the dots. Ask yourself very pointed questions and get to the bottom of your hurt feelings. This loss hurt your feelings for a reason; you need to understand why. Did you think that goal would bring more success? More status? Some validity within your profession? There is no wrong answer. The only thing that matters is that you can understand why it hurt.

Once you have written everything down as openly and honestly as possible, it's time to recover. This is when you give yourself some time to move on. Depending on the failure, you may need anywhere from a couple of hours to multiple weeks. It is important to move past the initial shock and start to feel better. The reason for this is to allow the emotions to subside so you can re-analyze the situation objectively.

Conduct the same level of analysis with your objective glasses on. Why do you think you failed this goal? What could you have done differently? Was it the right goal in the first place? What did you learn about yourself? What did you learn about the goal? How can you improve to be successful at a similar goal in the future? The more data you can pull from both perspectives, the more you can learn and grow.

## BE A FAILURE SCIENTIST

Think of yourself as a scientist conducting an experiment. You can even use the six steps of the scientific method to help create a reusable pattern.

1. **Ask a question.** What do I want to achieve? What is my goal?
2. **Do background research.** How will I achieve this goal? Who else has done it? What road maps do I have to follow? What will be required from me?
3. **Construct a hypothesis.** If (I do this), then (this) will happen. Create your action plan.
4. **Test your hypothesis by doing an experiment.** Move forward with your plan; you will either achieve your goal or fail.

5. **Analyze your data and draw a conclusion.** Whether you achieved your goal or not, you need the data for the next goal. Analyze what went wrong and what went right.
6. **Communicate your results.** What did we learn about ourselves, our journey, and our abilities? Now take that information and start over. You will get more refined with each attempt.

Taking a scientific approach forces us to analyze our failures and see them as opportunities instead of roadblocks. Imagine that your best friend were in your shoes and just failed the same way. What advice would you give your friend? How would you coach them through the situation and help them move forward? Assuming your heart is in the right place, your advice would likely be very sound.

That is because you are disconnected from your friend's failure. You didn't feel the sting they did. You are not emotionally engaged in what they have lost. You value your friend as a person, not as an achievement. You only care that they are growing from the experience. You want them to feel as good about themselves as you feel about them. This is the same response we are trying to have with our own failure.

To do that, we need to cope with the sting and the pain first. Then we can move on to the objective analysis and create a new action plan. When Albert Einstein (supposedly) said, "Insanity is doing the same thing over and over and expecting different results," I believe he was breaking down failure and achievement. We also know from Thomas Edison that one thousand attempts may be required to achieve a goal; therefore we may be required to try one thousand times without repeating the same mistakes.

That is how we succeed: by attempting as many times as necessary while never repeating an action that previously led to failure.

· · · · · · · · · · · · · · · · · · · · · · · · · · · · · · · · · ·

Life is hard. Failure is hard. Success is hard. We have already been through so much, so why continue to put ourselves through more? Why continue to push ourselves and face defeat and failure? Are we not fragile enough as it is?

I want to end this chapter with Theodore Roosevelt's famous quote about daring greatly. It is titled "It Is Not the Critic Who Counts," and I believe it answers a lot of these "whys."

> "It is not the critic who counts; not the man who points out how the strong man stumbles or where the doer of deeds could have done better. The credit belongs to the man who is actually in the arena, whose face is marred by dust and sweat and blood, who strives valiantly, who errs and comes up short again and again, because there is no effort without error or shortcoming, but who knows the great enthusiasms, the great devotions, who spends himself in a worthy cause; who, at the best, knows, in the end, the triumph of high achievement, and who, at the worst, if he fails, at least he fails while daring greatly, so that his place shall never be with those cold and timid souls who knew neither victory nor defeat." —Theodore Roosevelt, speech at the Sorbonne, Paris, April 23, 1910

To me, this speech outlines the courage it takes to try. Those who try are the ones in the arena, and they are the ones risking failure. They are the ones paving the way for future generations. They are knocking down roadblocks and putting up warning signs for those behind them. They are willing to go off the beaten path because it's where their heart is calling them. When you understand how powerful that is, you realize how insignificant the result (i.e., success or failure) really is. **You are not great because of what you have achieved; you are great because, despite everything, you keep trying.**

## Chapter 14

# SUCCESS, AND HOW TO DEFINE IT

> "The irony is that we attempt to disown our difficult stories, to appear more or less acceptable, but our wholeness— even our wholeheartedness—actually depends on the integration of all our experiences, including the falls."
> —**Brené Brown,** *Daring Greatly*

Success is something that people don't talk much about. We just assume that once we find it, we will be filled with happiness. The reality is that success is different for everyone. Oftentimes, we chase other people's definitions of it. If they want it, we must, too, right? Chasing someone else's definition of success will likely end with you being unfulfilled and hypercompetitive. By this point, you should acknowledge your gifts and fully understand the power you wield. Therefore, do not take that power lightly, and don't focus on things you don't truly want.

As you implement the lessons in this book, you will start to find success in your life. Some of you have never been told that before. It is vital that you are told how capable of success you really are. So many of the broken are discounted because of where we grew up or how we grew up. **Low expectations can and will affect your trajectory if you don't set your own high standards.**

This chapter will be about defining success. The only way we will ever feel successful is first to know what success looks like to us. But before we do that, it is important to acknowledge the power of expectations. The last thing I want is for someone to feel inspired by this book and ultimately not pursue change because of low expectations placed on them by themselves or others.

## THE POWER OF EXPECTATIONS

When I was living in Phelan, California, as a young boy, I constantly heard family members talk about how great it would be *if* I graduated high school. I remember them trying to encourage me, saying it would be such a great day *if* I could only graduate. I never thought about that expectation until I moved to New York to live with my dad. Suddenly, the talk around me was different. It was never "if" you graduate high school. It was "when" you graduate high school, you will start college.

I could feel the tension behind that new word, "when." And before I knew it, I was studying for the first time. I had to redo tenth grade because I failed too many classes, and now I was working my butt off to catch up and graduate "on time" a year late.

It wasn't until years later that I realized the power of these expectations. When my dad had a different expectation, I rose to the occasion. I graduated high school and started college right away. If I'd stayed in California, I would have dropped out of high school and had every intention of doing so. I could tell that people expected me to drop out because I was failing so badly. I knew deep down that it wouldn't shock anyone and they wouldn't care. I am not blaming my family for my failure, yet it is important to acknowledge the power of expectations. That way, those who are surrounded by people with low expectations of themselves and others are not so heavily influenced by their environments.

In 1964, a Harvard professor named Robert Rosenthal conducted an experiment at an elementary school. The experiment was conducted to determine the effect expectations had on children. According to his book *Pygmalion in the Classroom,* Rosenthal and his colleague led teachers in eighteen classrooms to believe that approximately 20 percent of their students were expected to bloom academically during the school year. The two then administered an IQ test schoolwide but renamed it the "Harvard Test of Inflected Acquisition." The students that were destined to bloom academically and intellectually were randomly selected.[39]

The students were tracked over the next two years. The students who were randomly selected as bloomers received higher praise from their teachers and increased gains in IQ. The test proved that when we expect certain things from ourselves and others, it changes the way we treat ourselves and others. The way we speak to them will change; the way we nurture them will change.

This is known as the Pygmalion effect, a self-fulfilling prophecy in which "a person's or a group's expectation for the behavior of another person or group serves actually to bring about the prophesied or expected behavior" as defined by the *Encyclopedia of Human Behavior*.[40] The prophecy goes as follows: Our beliefs about others influence our actions toward them. Our actions toward them influence their beliefs about themselves. Their beliefs about themselves influence their actions toward us, and the cycle continues.

Just as high expectations cause us to work harder and increase our performance, low expectations decrease our performance. This is known as the Golem Effect. If we understand the Golem Effect, we can avoid people who don't believe in us, and then create high expectations for ourselves. We can set the bar as high as we want. **It is up to us to believe in ourselves and not seek affirmation from those who expect too little.**

(On a side note, it is empowering to believe in others the way we desire to believe in ourselves. Not only does it feel good to identify greatness in others, but it can also help us figure out our own paths.)

## WHAT SUCCESS DOESN'T LOOK LIKE

Defining what success looks like to you is a very important step. The issue with success is that it is completely different for everyone. If you fail to define what success is for you, you may work your entire life toward something you don't want.

You could be chasing someone else's definition of success and find yourself miserable. Just because we hold certain professions in high regard does not mean you will be happy doing it. For example, when I talk to my friend who is an ER doctor, her workday makes me cringe. The politics that take place within hospitals are very similar to the politics that take place in police departments. Certain professions create mentalities and behaviors by making it difficult, if not impossible, to fire low-performing employees. This can create a very negative work environment, one that I never want to be part of again. Yet, to be a doctor is to make great money and be considered unanimously successful by society's standards.

Another profession regarded as the pinnacle of success is being a famous actor. Someone like Will Smith, Kevin Hart, or Dwayne Johnson . . . how great would that life be?! To me, horrible . . . I already have social anxiety from PTSD. Now imagine not being able to travel anywhere in the world without getting mauled by people. Everywhere you go someone is going to recognize you and try to touch you or talk to you. Someone is always waiting with a camera to try and push your buttons for a response. You become surrounded by a bubble of protection, never able to break that bubble without putting yourself or your family in danger. Yet there are people who would give up anything for that level of infamy.

The more you define what success looks like for you, the easier it will be to create that life for yourself. Without a clear definition, you will chase what society deems as success and just hope that it suits you.

Spend some time envisioning what your success looks like. Take the blinders off and let your imagination run wild. Do you want to own your own business? Do you want to be challenged regularly? Do you prefer autonomy, or would you prefer to be managed?

You may find that your dream is to live in the bush with no electricity, disconnected from society. Your dream may be to have a

Ferrari and live in Beverly Hills with celebrity neighbors. Whatever your dream is, defining it is the first step to obtaining it.

Our egos want us to achieve what other people deem as great—to prove to others that we have what it takes to obtain the things that *they* want. **The reality is, we will only find fulfillment and feel successful when we do what we are passionate about.**

Virgin Group founder and chairman Richard Branson earned his first million dollars at the age of twenty-three. Now worth over five billion dollars, this is what he had to say about success: "There is no greater thing you can do with your life and your work than follow your passions in a way that serves the world and you."

### Thoughts on Greatness

Greatness comes from singular obsessive focus. To singularly focus on something for enough time to become great, we need to be passionate. We need to find happiness in the act itself or spending ten thousand hours doing it will be a nightmare.

I can honestly say that at thirty-six years old, I have never been great at anything. I was a pretty good soldier but not great. I was a pretty good cop, but not a great one. Being great requires years, even decades, of singular focus. Anyone can be good, but to be great takes more time than most people are willing to spend. And it's always too much time when you are not passionate about what you do. Defining what your success is will align you with your true purpose. Only then will you be willing to put in enough time to become great.

> When I say that I have never been great at anything, I am also very proud of my willingness to move on. I recognized that greatness does not come from just doing one job for a long time. I knew that greatness would only come when I found the right job that could keep me engaged for decades. Too many of us are unwilling to change careers regardless of how misaligned they may feel. You cannot force your passion; you will get it wrong and that is okay. If you ever want to be great, you must be willing to move on when you know it's time. Sticking with a job because you've invested time in school, or because changing jobs will be difficult, is a mistake you will regret.

## ENVISIONING YOUR SUCCESS

The best part of having a clearly stated definition of success is that it prevents you from comparing yourself to others. If you know that freedom and time hold more value in your heart than materialism, then you will not be discouraged when someone else has materialistic things and you do not. You know that those things are not how you define success, and therefore there is no reason to compare. There is a saying, "If you don't stand for something, you'll fall for anything." If you don't define success for yourself, you will fall for everyone else's definition of it.

You can start figuring out what success looks like for you by using your imagination and your journal. Envision your future until you find one that scares you or seems too good to be true. Those are good indicators that your heart is aligned.

Nobody can compete with passion, and very few people choose careers based on passion alone. That will be your advantage. When you enter that career field, you are bringing skills from hardship and an aligned heart. With those two advantages, you will be your only real competition.

Envisioning your future does more than just help you determine what path to follow. It starts to solidify the standard you are setting for yourself. It gives your mind its direction and purpose to aim for with every decision you make. You are showing your mind the desired future and reinforcing it with the chemicals that flood your body when you feel good thinking about it. Steve Harvey said, "Imagination is everything; it's the preview to life's coming attractions." That is how powerful the mind is. **When you imagine what you desire with great detail and believe that you can achieve it, your body and mind will work as a cohesive unit to move you toward that goal.**

Just like the teachers in Rosenthal's experiment, when we believe someone is special, we treat them differently. We work harder to nurture their creativity, we trust their opinions and beliefs more, and they get special treatment. When you know that *you* are special because of your past, your ambition, and your value as a person, your actions toward yourself and your situation will change. You will be able to label yourself a bloomer just like the teachers labeled those kids. The only difference is your bloomer status will be based on fact and not fiction.

## MIND MAPPING

One technique to help you discover what success looks like for you is called mind mapping. It is a form of journaling that better replicates your brain's thought patterns. To mind map, you simply start with a basic theme, so in this case, "success." You write "success" in the center of a blank sheet of paper. From there, you let your imagination dictate how you add to that word. The point of this exercise is to find your passion while avoiding strict, linear note-taking that is better suited for goals and plans of action.

You don't even have to write the word "success" if success is better represented to you as a picture. If that's the case, draw that picture. From there, any idea that reminds you of success or comes to mind while thinking about success will be connected by a line. I use this technique when I hit a wall in my thinking process. I don't put any requirements or expectations on it. At times I'll have a breakthrough and connect multiple dots in my desires and thought patterns, and other times I will get nothing. If I get nothing, I will hang the final product on a wall or put it on my desk for a few days. I know that the page is full of data that I have yet to work out in my mind; it just needs time to develop.

Like a toddler scribbling, it will look nonsensical and disorganized. Don't try and make sense of it in the moment. Just let the thoughts roll from your brain and be represented on the paper. Once your diagram starts to form, you will see connections and be able to evaluate your work.

The process of mind mapping is a great tool for figuring out your desires when you just can't pinpoint what you want or why. The more you allow your mind to wander, the deeper into your subconscious you will get. So many of our thoughts and ideas are dictated by what we currently think is possible. This exercise can help you to think past those mental limitations and tap into your true desires. You are developing the ability to think deeply.

## A VISION BOARD

Another tool that can help you discover your definition of success is a vision board. Not because you think the universe will read it and grant you three wishes, but because it helps to solidify your desired future and make it a reality. Once again, we are utilizing the power of neuroplasticity to rewire our brains for success. Marla Tabaka, writing for *Inc.* magazine, said that this rewiring process harnesses mirror neurons and neural resonance. Mirror neurons are key to learning and planning our actions, "as well as understanding the intentions behind them." Meanwhile, neural resonance helps with focus and problem-solving. In short, "Visualization can help us to rewire our brains resulting in greater access to ideas, solutions, and motivation."[41]

Most people wander lost in this world not because they lack the skill or ability to achieve their dreams, but because they never clearly defined what their dreams were.

So, what is a vision board and how will it help? A vision board is a collage of pictures that are utilized to represent your passions and desires in life. Vision boards have been used by people like Curtis

Jackson (aka 50 Cent), Oprah Winfrey, and Beyoncé, and according to a TD Bank survey of over five hundred small businesses, one in five successful entrepreneurs.[42] The goal of the board is twofold: Firstly, to keep you focused on the things you want. Secondly, to define what those things are. This is another chance to break down the limitations you have placed on your brain and tap in to what truly motivates you.

My vision board has a picture of a 1963 Chevrolet Impala, a cabin in the Colorado mountains, a BJJ black belt, books, and my family. My board is not complete, but it connects me to what is important in this phase of my life. I no longer care about being the best in my field or earning the respect of others. I am in a phase where I want the luxury of family time and beautiful scenery. I want to pursue personal achievements more than professional ones. I want to stay connected to my roots with classic cars instead of fancy new ones. I want to educate myself simply for the sake of doing so—with no other purpose than to enjoy good literature, ideas, and concepts.

Just as important as the pictures you put on your vision board are the things that don't make the list. Are you spending time and energy on things that don't even qualify for your board? I have obsessively focused on aspects of my life that didn't make it. Knowing this allows me to redirect and re-concentrate my efforts on more meaningful endeavors.

* * *

I must constantly redefine what I want, and why I want it, because I never want to miss my target. I always want to know what my target is. I would be devastated if I spent one more minute living for the approval of others. Define what success looks like for you. Learn to use your imagination to paint the perfect picture.

Your mind is an architect, one of the best in the world. It can build anything in existence if given the chance. Allow your mind to do what it does and create your desired future. Once it has done that, your body and actions will follow. It's not magic; it's not hopes and wishes. We are just imagining our best lives and then working toward building them. None of this happens without constant and consistent action. Once you have identified your target, then it is time to take aim.

## Chapter 15

# CONSISTENCY / BUILDING HABITS

*"Success isn't always about greatness. It's about consistency. Consistent hard work leads to success. Greatness will come."*
—**Dwayne "The Rock" Johnson**

Consistency is a cruel, repetitive requirement for success. It is not enough to do difficult things infrequently. They must be done regularly and consistently to see long-term results. This makes the process nearly unbearable for the ones who are not truly committed. This is what will separate those who use their gifts from those who squander them.

The final step in transitioning from a life of poverty to success is consistency. This is the hardest part of your transition for a variety of reasons. This is the step that separates good from great, achievers from non-achievers. This is where you continue to journal, avoid negativity, pursue your passions, define success, and keep pushing despite your motivation subsiding. Consistency is the pill that nobody wants to swallow. We are ambitious, we are hungry, we are passionate, but are we committed? We would work our fingers to the bone and avoid sleep at all costs if it would lead us to immediate success.

Even though at times it will seem like nothing is working, you will need to trust the process and continue to put in the hard work to succeed. Everyone has a point in their life when they become motivated to change and grow. Yet most of them will stop the positive actions the minute they no longer feel motivated. **The key is to know that motivation is a temporary feeling designed to help you get started.** Nobody can sustain their initial motivation level without it declining at some point or another.

Therefore, it is important to know that the feeling of motivation is not accurate for long-term success. No matter how passionate you are, when the work gets tough, your passion will feel like a job. You will feel your motivation decline, and you must stick with your plan and continue to work toward your goals.

## COMPLETE YOUR MISSION

This is where the Special Operations mindset kicks in. Despite not feeling motivated, I have already created a game plan to get from my current position to my desired one. The plan is my mission—I must complete my mission at all costs. Why? Because I told myself I would. The minute I tell myself I will do something and fail to do it, I lose trust in my ability to commit. I will no longer believe myself when

I set out to achieve a goal. If I don't believe in myself, Rosenthal's Pygmalion effect and the law of attraction will be rendered useless.

We must believe wholeheartedly in our willingness to see every single goal through to the end. If you do not believe in yourself, you will know it subconsciously. Your body will not make the necessary changes to obtain your goals because it knows deep down that you will give up. Yet when you know with 100 percent certainty that you will commit, your body will change to avoid humiliation.

When you commit regardless of the outcome, your body and mind will work together to avoid a total disaster. You will rise to the occasion as though a primitive survival instinct has taken over. Your mind and body will react to the potential humiliation as though it means exile from a tribe and ultimately death. You will start to fear the negative outcomes more than you are excited about the positive ones. This fear will encourage preparation so you can have a fighting chance.

As the saying goes, "showing up is half the battle." Getting to the starting line can be the hardest part of achieving a goal. The morning I was set to fly out to Special Forces Selection, fear overtook my body. I had zero desire to get on that plane. I would have welcomed any excuse to avoid the trip and claim it wasn't my fault. The only reason I got on the plane was because I signed up and I had to complete my mission. I had to see it through to the end; otherwise, all the anxiety and preparation would be for nothing. I knew that once the fear had subsided, I would be filled with regret if I quit. I got on that plane, faced my fear, and got told I was selected at the end of the hardest three weeks of my life.

**Quitting is the absence of achievement without the lessons of failure.**

## THE FINAL PHASE

The journey has been intense. Always having to readjust your perception of yourself and your environment. Ridding your life of negativity. Endless self-education through self-help books and podcasts. Learning how to cope with failure and using it to your advantage. The list goes on, but everything you did had something in common. You were always able to start working on things the minute you discovered them.

The very second you heard of a good book, you pulled out your phone and downloaded it. The second you decided to obtain a formal education, you contacted the school and made an appointment. When you wanted a challenge, you got online and signed up for a half marathon, or a marathon.

Everything that has gotten you this far has been about creating a plan of attack, then attacking. Now that you have gotten 95 percent there, now that you are doing all the habits that create success and you are one step away from obtaining your dreams, the final piece of advice is . . . **just keep doing what you are doing**.

I have heard that advice with every profession or endeavor I have ever set out to achieve. I hate that advice with every ounce of my being. I don't want to just keep doing what I'm doing. I want to do more so I can become successful faster. I want to bypass the time required for greatness with hard work and dedication. I am seeking advice because I am looking for the final piece of the puzzle. Every time I knew that "time" was the final factor in my growth, I would fight it. There must be a way to grow at a faster pace, to achieve what I want sooner. With every attempt to change the rules, I would find myself in the same spot, getting the same answer: "Just . . . keep . . .

doing . . . what you're doing." I could scream in that moment. I am overwhelmed with motivation and desire to achieve—how can I not push through this barrier?

Why is it that we struggle so much with this final phase? Why is time and consistency such a difficult concept to embrace? One reason is that we know our motivation will not last. We also know that the desire to push as hard as possible is not sustainable. There will come a day when we no longer want to work that hard, or doing so detracts from other life goals. This causes us to feel the pressure to get as far as possible before that motivation wanes and the real work begins.

## WHEN GREATNESS HAPPENS

The reality is that greatness happens long after the motivation wanes. It is easy to chase something you are momentarily passionate about. Those who know greatness chased that passion far beyond that point. Muhammad Ali said, "I don't count my sit-ups; I only start counting when it starts hurting because they're the only ones that count."

Muhammad Ali understood what it took to be great. He knew that the real work started when things got difficult. Yet many people do not expect patience to be the most difficult challenge. I have zero patience and have had to learn it the hard way. Once I have done all I can do to increase my chances of success and the only thing left is to consistently repeat those actions, that is when things get hard for me.

That is when self-doubt reenters my mental space. I become overwhelmed with questions: How long will it take? Should I be doing more? Did I do enough? Those questions lead to looking at others to compare my progress with theirs. It is the start of a dip in my mental health. I have learned to recognize that dip so I can pull myself out of it. To recover, I turn off the social media and focus on my vision board and my definition of success, neither of which has anything about being the most successful entrepreneur, or anything to do with accolades at all for that matter. So why am I comparing myself to others? I don't even want what they have.

Ali also said, "It isn't the mountains ahead to climb that wear you out: it's the pebble in your shoe."

The pebble in my shoe is patience. The only way to overcome my lack of patience is by committing to my goals whether I feel motivated or not. When I decide I want to achieve something, I go to my journal and create a plan. Once that plan is created, I see it through to the end no matter what.

• • • • • • • • • • • • • • • • • • • • • • • •

A great example of the difficulty of consistency is a phenomenon in Brazilian Jiu-Jitsu called the "blue belt blues." It happens to newly promoted blue belts who have finally achieved their goal of no longer being white belts. They are suddenly saddened by the piece of advice that comes along with obtaining a blue belt, *just keep doing what you are doing*, and often quit BJJ altogether. A blue belt is a BJJ practitioner who has learned enough of the foundational principles to start adding techniques and variations to their game. In other words, they are past most of the monumental improvements that come with being new.

From that point, improvement will be mostly small, incremental adjustments to their game. The light at the end of the tunnel suddenly runs away and you're left with nothing to focus on but the work.

So many people are motivated as white belts solely to obtain the coveted colored belt. Once they do, they no longer have the energy, focus, and motivation to start the process all over again. They are hyper-focused on a peak, and when they get there, the absence of that peak demoralizes them.

It's fun to watch new white belts come into class. They will be at every single class, every single day, and sometimes even twice a day. You weren't there to check, but they are happy to inform you of how many times they have trained that week.

It is fun to watch because you know that their motivation will subside. You will then determine who will make it past the blue belt blues by how many times they show up once they no longer have that peak to focus on. Once they realize that they have learned the foundational principles and all they have left to do is keep training, it is no longer exciting. Yet some people will show up anyway; they have committed to BJJ regardless of belt color or how they feel about training. They consistently show up to class and learn despite not feeling like it or seeing drastic improvements. Then suddenly the floodgates open and all the hours spent on the mats click. They seem to go from good to great overnight.

## OUR CENTRAL PATTERN GENERATORS

**You can never find consistency when you base your actions on how you feel.** Our emotions are the furthest thing from consistency. We change how we feel from one minute to the next. We can't rely on our emotions to determine our actions. Once we have a plan, we stick with that plan no matter what. We see it through to success or failure. We will either learn from the failure or reinforce our actions from success. Quitting is the only way to rob yourself of a positive outcome.

Stanford professor and neuroscientist Andrew Huberman had this to say about consistency: "Sometimes we want to see the physical or the financial results right away, but I think a big part of it is that you're training your nervous system. We have central pattern generators, which are neurons that are in our spinal cord and brain stem that generate repetitive movements. The brain loves to load central pattern generators with work because then the mind can think about other things."[43]

Our goal with consistency is to get as many of the lessons in this book as possible into our central pattern generators so they become second nature. We don't want to spend all our time thinking about positive behaviors and having to work tirelessly to implement change. We want to free up that mental energy to enjoy life and feel the reward of all the hard work.

So how do you overcome the decline of motivation and continue to push toward your goals? How do you become so consistent that your actions become second nature, freeing up your ability to think about bigger challenges? My answer to that question is this—just keep doing what you are doing.

There is no cheat code; there is no hack to overcome the final phase of success. If you are implementing positive changes in your life, and short bursts of motivation have gotten you into the gym, training in martial arts, reading books, or going to college, then the only answer is to keep going, regardless of how you feel.

You will need to rely on the tactics taught in this book to overcome the lack of motivation. Rely on your vision board. Write your "why" down for every goal, and look at it every day. Get in your journal and document your decline in motivation. Keep data on how you feel when and why. Only then will you be able to adjust the formula and find what works for you. Does a certain author get you fired up? Is there a motivational podcast that can get you through a hump? Do you have a friend or spouse who can help motivate and push you?

## TOMORROW WILL WORRY ABOUT ITSELF

When I was going through the Special Forces Qualification Course, I had to rely heavily on the men around me. Kurt was with me the entire way; he became one of my best friends and is now a co-owner of The FNG Academy. I remember one day I was literally afraid of what we were about to do in the field. We were about to set off on a training foot patrol and camp for multiple nights. The issue was that the North Carolina winter was brutal. The news kept giving it names like "arctic blast," which really didn't help my mental state.

As I sat in the bottom bunk dreading the next day, Kurt looked down from the top bunk and read a quote from the Bible that he had found. It was Matthew 6:34 (NIV), and it read, "Therefore do not worry about tomorrow, for tomorrow will worry about itself."

That one sentence in that pivotal moment pulled me out of a downward spiral. I started to focus on how good it was to be in a warm bed in that moment. I stopped worrying about what was to come and focused on the present. To this day, I remember that moment far more than I remember the frigid temperatures that followed.

We are never in this alone. It is encouraged to seek help from those in your inner circle. When you are feeling down, seek out a trusted friend. It is not a weakness. It is wisdom to understand your limitations and courage to ask for help.

If you want to transition into success, then know that your motivation will wane. Have a plan to stay consistent when that happens and never back down out of fear or lack of desire. Get those positive habits into your central pattern generator and success will become second nature.

# Chapter 16

# BUILD THE LIFE YOU WANT

"Character cannot be developed in ease and quiet. Only through experience of trial and suffering can the soul be strengthened, ambition inspired, and success achieved."
**—Helen Keller**

We deserve to live the life of our dreams. We were gifted trauma as children. We were gifted trauma as soldiers, police officers, paramedics. It is up to us to use that gift for good. When we help ourselves transition from success in poverty to societal success, we can then do the most rewarding thing on the planet: help other people.

During an episode of the *Jordan B Peterson Podcast* featuring neuroscientist and Stanford professor Andrew Huberman and clinical psychologist Jordan Peterson, Huberman discussed how some people's brains process information differently during autonomic arousal or stress. He states that based on neuroimaging, "the prefrontal cortex is essentially leading the response of the anterior cingulate cortex (ACC) and the insula. Information is coming up from the body and into the insula, then being fed to the prefrontal cortex, which allows the prefrontal cortex to lead the response like the coach of a team."

This is the ideal brain process in a high-stress situation. Our prefrontal cortex can regulate our thoughts, emotions, and actions appropriately based on the situation at hand. But what about those of us who are not choosing the most appropriate responses? What if our trauma is causing a dysfunctional response from the prefrontal cortex, taking our brains unnecessarily into survival mode and leaving us filled with guilt and shame?

Professor Huberman goes on to explain that in people with chronic anxiety or prefrontal cortex damage, the order is reversed. The insula and ACC lead and direct the response of the prefrontal cortex. "People then default to one primitive rule set, which may or may not be the appropriate response."

Huberman mentions Special Operations soldiers and how this response is where their power lies. When things become extremely stressful, their primitive rule set can often be the most appropriate response. Therefore, they can make the best decision possible regardless of the height of their autonomic arousal. Finally, he discusses how this response can work against us in other career fields.

*In a really good debate, you can't allow the autonomic response to overtake you, or you lose access to an enormous database that resides in one's hippocampus and you default to the bodily state, which is what we see when we see people become dysregulated with rage.*

Huberman may have highlighted the transition from poverty and hardship to success. When growing up in rough and unforgiving neighborhoods, your basic instincts could be the most appropriate response. In those environments, your ability to respond swiftly and aggressively could save your life. Like Special Operations soldiers, you were conditioned to act when others would freeze. Unfortunately, those responses are rarely acceptable in other professional scenarios. Once we can transition those autonomic responses to be appropriate in a professional setting, we become unstoppable.

The answer is implementing positive habits and allowing neuroplasticity to rewire our brains, while simultaneously training our nervous systems to load central pattern generators with as many positive habits as possible. The more we automate positive behaviors, the quicker and easier appropriate responses become.

· · · · · · · · · · · · · · · · · · · · · · · · · · · · · · · ·

By implementing the advice in this book, you will start to feel and respond differently to nearly everything in your life.

Soon it will seem to others as though success follows you. People will want to know your secret and wonder how you are able to achieve one thing after another. You will tell them about the positive habits you have developed and the hard work required to be consistent. If they are already implementing positive habits, you will give them the dreaded advice, "Just keep doing what you are doing." They may feel the advice is unfulfilling or shallow, but you know that it is the best advice anyone can give. That statement holds the key to winning.

Nobody can persevere like the broken. The broken have had to push through pain and suffering that most could only imagine, often doing so as children. Our hardships were once our greatest weaknesses. Left unchecked, they hindered our ability to function appropriately in society. We developed triggers that prevented us from doing daily tasks that others did with ease. Focusing on what we failed to do caused us to feel like being broken was a curse and that we were destined for failure.

Yet, deep down, we want more out of life. We want to transcend our past and seek fulfillment. The last thing any of us want is to perpetuate abuse. We want to break the cycle. So we distance ourselves from our past. We suppress our memories and pretend to be people we are not. Yet no matter how far we run from our past, we stay connected. The further we get, the more we become aware of the negative effects of our trauma.

It's not until we learn to run toward our past that we can reconcile and learn from it. We must face the bad to unlock the good. I was able to do that by journaling my life from beginning to end, documenting all the moments that stood out to me. That journal ended up becoming my first book, *Rising Above*.

The process was healing in that it allowed me to make peace with those who inflicted the most pain. I could understand their pain and the decisions that led them down that path. I was able to connect the pain of my past to my best attributes. That is when I realized that hardship was my greatest teacher. It was the trauma that gave me the ability to be great. **Everything about trauma made me better, stronger, and more resilient. Those who experience trauma are like diamonds formed from the pressure of pain and struggle.**

The broken are special and need to know it in order to pursue the greatness they deserve. To transition into greatness, outward habits need to reflect inward potential. You need to choose to act in a way that reflects who you can be and not where you came from.

And so now it is time to start living the life you want to live. You owe it to yourself to create the environment you wished you had growing up. Some wished for peace within their homes. Some wished they had people in their homes who cared for and nurtured them.

Whatever it is that you wish you had, now is your time to create that for yourself. Now is the time to change your lineage, to rewrite your stories, and start perpetuating greatness through your bloodline. We can't change the past, and after reading this book, I hope that you wouldn't want to. What we can do is start being the change we always prayed for. We do that by using our hardships to find happiness.

We show people that no matter the circumstance, we can live out our dreams and this world can be an absolute blessing. I thank God every day that I wake up and get to spend it with my family and friends. I have cultivated a dream life that makes me happy. It is not always easy; at times my triggers still make things hard for me and everyone around me. But we all love each other and work hard to cultivate our bonds and grow together. My oldest daughter just made honor roll; I was never close to honor roll in my life. I am watching abuse cycles end in my family, and our story—my story—is being rewritten. Now it will be one of success, love, and encouragement.

I work with my best friends, and we get to help people every day. For the first time in my life, I truly love what I do—so much so that I would do it for free. My wife is my best friend and the best wife a man could ask for.

Our dreams can come true, and we deserve to live them. We have earned the right to be happy and know what greatness feels like. To achieve this, we must have the courage to follow our hearts and be disciplined to complete our goals. Nothing great ever comes easy. You shouldn't want it to; it is the struggle that makes everything so much sweeter.

You have suffered, you have been tried, your soul has been strengthened, your ambition has been inspired. Now it is time for your success to be achieved.

My final advice on your path to success is to aim at a particular target, one that I think every broken person should aim for. This particular target should be a goal within all of us who have endured and survived hardship. Help others. Fulfillment for achievers will always be found in putting others before ourselves.

Friedrich Nietzsche said, "To live is to suffer, to survive is to find some meaning in the suffering." We are survivors, and we owe it to every broken man, woman, and child to pass our abilities on. Give away the tools that helped you find meaning. If you think achieving your dreams feels good, wait till you help someone else achieve theirs. That is when the circle completes itself. That is when we truly experience the meaning in our suffering.

There is no better definition of success. There is no greater purpose than that. Create your own path to greatness and achieve as many things that are meaningful to you as possible. Once you have done that, help others do the same.

> "Anywhere I see suffering, that is where I want to be, doing what I can."
> **–Princess Diana**

# NOTES

1. American SPCC (n.d.). *Child Maltreatment Statistics*. Retrieved April 1, 2022, from https://americanspcc.org/child-maltreatment-statistics/.
2. CDC (2022, April 6). *Preventing Child Abuse & Neglect*. https://www.cdc.gov/violenceprevention/pdf/can/CAN-factsheet_2022.pdf.
3. CDC (2022, April 6). *Fast Facts: Preventing Adverse Childhood Experiences*. https://www.cdc.gov/violenceprevention/aces/fastfact.html.
4. Jung, C. G. (1938). In CW 11: Psychology and Religion: West and East. P.131
5. Stern, C. (2021, April 29). *Oprah details horrific abuse she faced as a child, revealing she was regularly "whupped" by her grandmother—and forced to sleep on the PORCH by a boarding house owner who didn't want a "nappy-headed dark child" inside*. https://www.dailymail.co.uk/femail/article-9525681/Oprah-details-childhood-abuse-revealing-grandma-whupped-regularly.html.
6. Coelho, Paulo. 1995. *The Alchemist*. London, England: Thorsons.
7. American SPCC (n.d.). Child Maltreatment Statistics. Retrieved April 1, 2022, from https://americanspcc.org/child-maltreatment-statistics/.
8. Taylor, S. E., Pham, L. B., Rivkin, I. D., & Armor, D. A. (1998). Harnessing the imagination. Mental simulation, self-regulation, and coping. *The American Psychologist*, 53(4), 429–439. https://doi.org/10.1037//0003-066x.53.4.429.
9. Rozin, P., & Royzman, E. B. (2001). Negativity bias, negativity dominance, and contagion. *Personality and Social Psychology Review*, 5(4), 296–320.
10. Rozin, P., & Royzman, E. B. (2001). Negativity bias, negativity dominance, and contagion. *Personality and Social Psychology Review*, 5(4), 296–320.
11. Amen, D. (2019, October 17). *How Negative Thoughts Affect Brain Health + What to Do About Them*. Mind Body Green, https://www.mindbodygreen.com/articles/how-negative-thoughts-affect-brain-health-what-to-do-about-them.
12. Greene, R. (2010). *The 50th Law*. London, England: Profile Books.
13. Gabay, R., Hameiri, B., Rubel-Lifschitz, T., & Nadler, A. (2020). The tendency for interpersonal victimhood: The personality construct and its consequences. *Personality and Individual Differences*, 165, Article 110134.

## NOTES

14. Gabay, R., Hameiri, B., Rubel-Lifschitz, T., & Nadler, A. (2020). The tendency for interpersonal victimhood: The personality construct and its consequences. *Personality and Individual Differences, 165*, Article 110134.
15. Kaufman, S. B. (2020). Unraveling the Mindset of Victimhood. *Scientific American*. https://www.scientificamerican.com/article/unraveling-the-mindset-of-victimhood/.
16. Kaufman, S. B. (2020). Unraveling the Mindset of Victimhood. *Scientific American*. https://www.scientificamerican.com/article/unraveling-the-mindset-of-victimhood/.
17. Tambiah, S. J. (2019). The Weberian Dualities. *Comparative Social Dynamics: Essays in Honor of SN Eisenstadt*.
18. Tedeschi, R. G., & Calhoun, L. G. (2004). "Posttraumatic growth: Conceptual foundations and empirical evidence." *Psychological Inquiry, 15*(1), 1–18.
19. American SPCC (n.d.). Child Maltreatment Statistics. Retrieved April 1, 2022, from https://americanspcc.org/child-maltreatment-statistics/.
20. Heim, C., Mletzko, T., Purselle, D., Musselman, D. L., & Nemeroff, C. B. (2008). The dexamethasone/corticotropin-releasing factor test in men with major depression: Role of childhood trauma. *Biological Psychiatry*, 63: 398–405.
21. Hankins, S., Hoekstra, M., & Skiba, P. M. (2011). The Ticket to Easy Street? The Financial Consequences of Winning the Lottery. *The Review of Economics and Statistics*, 93 (3): 961–969. doi: https://doi.org/10.1162/REST_a_00114.
22. Al Odhayani, A., Watson, W. J., & Watson, L. (2013). Behavioural consequences of child abuse. *Can Fam Physician*, 59(8): 831–836. PMID: 23946022; PMCID: PMC3743691.
23. Digiulio, S. (2018, July 22). *Why 'getting lost in a book' is so good for you, according to science*. Nbcnews.com. Retrieved May 25, 2023, from https://www.nbcnews.com/better/pop-culture/why-getting-lost-book-so-good-you-according-science-ncna893256.
24. Oatley, K., & Peterson, J. B. (2009). Exploring the link between reading fiction and empathy: Ruling out individual differences and examining outcomes. *Communications*. https://doi.org/10.1515/Comm.2009.025.
25. Heim, C., Mletzko, T., Purselle, D., Musselman, D. L., & Nemeroff, C. B. (2008). The dexamethasone/corticotropin-releasing factor test in men with major depression: Role of childhood trauma. *Biological Psychiatry*, 63: 398–405.
26. Tseng, J., & Poppenk, J. (2020). Brain meta-state transitions demarcate thoughts across task contexts exposing the mental noise of trait neuroticism. *Nature Communications*, 11(1), 1–12.
27. Koschwanez, H. E., Kerse, N., Darragh, M., Jarrett, P., Booth, R. J., & Broadbent, E. (2013). Expressive writing and wound healing in older adults: a randomized controlled trial. *Psychosom Med*, 75(6): 581–590. doi: 10.1097/PSY.0b013e31829b7b2e. Epub 2013, June 26. PMID: 23804013.
28. Grothaus, M. (2015, January 29). Why Journaling Is Good for Your Health (And 8 Tips to Get Better). Fast Company. https://www.fastcompany.com/3041487/8-tips-to-more-effective-journaling-for-health.

29  Grothaus, M. (2015, January 29). Why Journaling Is Good for Your Health (And 8 Tips to Get Better). Fast Company. https://www.fastcompany.com/3041487/8-tips-to-more-effective-journaling-for-health.
30  Moran, J. (2013). Pause, reflect and give thanks: The power of gratitude during the holidays. *UCLA Newsroom*. https://doi.org/2013.
31  Hackney, A. C. (2006). Stress and the neuroendocrine system: the role of exercise as a stressor and modifier of stress. *Expert Rev Endocrinol Metab*, 1(6):783–792. doi: 10.1586/17446651.1.6.783. PMID: 20948580; PMCID: PMC2953272.
32  Suzuki, W. (2021, October 22). *A neuroscientist shares the 4 brain-changing benefits of exercise—And how much she does every week*. CNBC. Retrieved May 23, 2023, from https://www.cnbc.com/2021/10/22/neuroscientist-shares-the-brain-health-benefits-of-exercise-and-how-much-she-does-a-week.html.
33  Omasu, F., Hotta, Y., Watanabe, M., & Yoshioka, T. (2018). The Relationship between Post-Traumatic Stress Disorder and Self-Esteem along with the Importance of Support for Children. *Open Journal of Preventive Medicine*, 8(04), 95.
34  Markway, B. (2018). Why Self-Confidence Is More Important Than You Think. *Psychology Today*. https://doi.org/09/20/2018.
35  Balcetis, E., Riccio, M. T., Duncan, D. T., Cole, S. (2019, July 19). Keeping the Goal in Sight: Testing the Influence of Narrowed Visual Attention on Physical Activity. *Personality and Social Psychology Bulletin*, 46(3), 485–496. https://doi.org/10.1177/0146167219861438.
36  Smith, E. N., Young, M. D., Crum, A. J. (2020, January 15). Stress, Mindsets, and Success in Navy SEALs Special Warfare Training. *Frontiers in Psychology*, 10. https://doi.org/10.3389/fpsyg.2019.02962.
37  Keller, G., & Papasan, J. (2012). *The One Thing: The Surprisingly Simple Truth Behind Extraordinary Results*. Austin, TX: Bard Press.
38  Henry Miller Quotes. (n.d.). BrainyQuote.com. Retrieved June 3, 2023, from BrainyQuote.com website: https://www.brainyquote.com/quotes/henry_miller_133854
39  Rosenthal, R., & Jacobson, L. (1968). Pygmalion in the classroom. The urban review, 3(1), 16-20.
40  Encyclopedia of Human Behavior. (2012). Netherlands: Elsevier Science.
41  Tabaka, M. (2019, December 2). A new study shows 1 in 5 successful entrepreneurs use vision boards. Inc. https://www.inc.com/marla-tabaka/study-shows-1-in-5-successful-entrepreneurs-use-vision-boards-backed-by-neuroscience.html.
42  Bank, T. (2016, January 20). Visualizing Goals Influences Financial Health and Happiness, Study Finds. PR News Wire. https://www.prnewswire.com/news-releasesvisualizing-goals-influences-financial-health-and-happiness-study-finds-300207028.html.
43  Huberman, A., & Hyman, M. "My Daily Hacks to Improve Sleep, Destroy Laziness & Live Longer!" The Doctor's Farmacy. Podcast. July 14, 2021. https://www.youtube.com/watch?v=4aLjJM2HFXs.

# ABOUT THE AUTHOR

Sean "Buck" Rogers is a best-selling author, former Green Beret, and law enforcement officer. Born in Phelan, California, Buck refused to allow his childhood trauma to shape his future and utilized his past to obtain fulfillment in life. After joining the military, he always strived for more. Buck went to Ranger selection, and despite getting hurt in the course, it taught him many lessons he later used for Special Forces Selection and earned his Green Beret. Buck continued to hone his mental toughness through running and education; having run multiple ultramarathons and earning a master's degree, Buck continues to strive for greatness. He finished his career serving the Denver Police Department and is constantly helping others achieve more through his company the FNG Academy.